CERTIFIED VMWARE VSPHERE 8.X PROFESSIONAL EXAM PREP 2025

Unlock 180+ Practice Questions, Detailed Answer Explanations, and Prep Tips

George Hackett

ALL RIGHTS RESERVED @ 2025

TABLE OF CONTENT

INTRODUCTION

VMware vSphere is a leading virtualization platform that enables organizations to consolidate, manage, and scale virtual infrastructures efficiently. As businesses increasingly adopt cloud computing, vSphere provides the foundation for modern data centers by allowing physical hardware to be virtualized and resources shared across multiple virtual machines (VMs). By abstracting computing, storage, and networking resources, VMware vSphere supports the rapid deployment of applications, reduces capital costs, and enhances business agility.

At its core, VMware vSphere allows organizations to create virtualized environments that provide the flexibility and efficiency needed for today's fast-paced IT landscape. The platform consists of several components designed to streamline the management of virtual infrastructure, support high availability, and ensure optimal resource allocation.

The Role of vSphere in Virtualization

Virtualization is the process of creating a virtual version of something, such as a server, storage device, or network, instead of relying solely on physical infrastructure. VMware vSphere leverages this technology to enable organizations to maximize the use of their physical servers by running multiple VMs on a single hardware host.

By virtualizing the server layer, vSphere enables IT administrators to manage multiple workloads on fewer physical machines, which reduces hardware costs and energy consumption. This consolidation is particularly beneficial for data centers, where reducing the physical footprint of servers leads to significant cost savings and more efficient use of space.

Key Components of VMware vSphere

VMware vSphere 8.x builds upon the robust architecture of previous versions by offering new features that improve performance, scalability, and security. To fully understand the platform, it's essential to become familiar with its primary components:

VMware ESXi: The ESXi hypervisor is the backbone of vSphere, allowing multiple VMs to run on a single physical server. ESXi abstracts the underlying hardware resources and allocates them to the VMs, making it possible to optimize the use of CPU, memory, storage, and network bandwidth. ESXi is a bare-metal hypervisor, meaning it is installed directly on the server hardware without requiring an underlying operating system, reducing overhead and improving performance.

vCenter Server: vCenter Server is the centralized management tool for vSphere environments. It provides a single interface to manage all ESXi hosts, virtual networks, storage, and VMs. vCenter Server allows administrators to perform critical tasks such as provisioning VMs, monitoring performance, automating workflows, and implementing disaster recovery solutions. With vSphere 8.x, vCenter Server **benefits from simplified lifecycle management, enhanced scalability, and improved performance monitoring tools.**

> **VMware vSphere Distributed Services Engine (DPU):** A new feature introduced in vSphere 8.x, the Distributed Services Engine offloads certain network and storage tasks to Data Processing Units (DPUs), freeing up CPU resources for application workloads. This enhancement improves overall system performance and reduces latency, making vSphere 8.x particularly well-suited for modern cloud-native applications and data-intensive workloads.

> **vSphere High Availability (HA):** This feature ensures that critical applications remain available in case of hardware failures. HA continuously monitors ESXi hosts and, in the event of a failure, automatically restarts VMs on other available hosts within the cluster. This capability significantly reduces downtime and ensures business continuity.

> **vSphere Distributed Resource Scheduler (DRS):** DRS automates the distribution of computing resources across a cluster of ESXi hosts. By continuously monitoring resource usage and balancing workloads, DRS optimizes performance and ensures that VMs have the resources they need to operate efficiently. This is especially useful in environments with fluctuating workloads, as it minimizes manual intervention and ensures optimal resource allocation.

Significance of VMware vSphere 8.x

vSphere 8.x represents a significant upgrade over previous versions, introducing new features and enhancements that cater to the evolving needs of modern IT environments. One of the most notable advancements is the Distributed Services Engine, which addresses the performance limitations associated with traditional CPU-centric architectures. By offloading certain tasks to DPUs, vSphere 8.x optimizes the use of system resources, allowing organizations to handle more complex and data-intensive workloads.

Additionally, vSphere 8.x includes improvements in lifecycle management, making it easier for administrators to update and manage ESXi hosts and vCenter Server. This streamlined management process reduces the complexity of maintaining large-scale virtual environments and minimizes downtime during system upgrades.

Another key improvement is the expanded support for Kubernetes through vSphere with Tanzu, which enables organizations to run containerized applications alongside traditional VMs on the same platform. This integration provides a unified platform for both legacy applications and modern, cloud-native workloads, making vSphere 8.x an ideal solution for enterprises looking to embrace DevOps practices and hybrid cloud architectures.

Practical Examples of vSphere's Impact on Data Centers

VMware vSphere has become the standard for virtualization in enterprise data centers, providing businesses with the tools to maximize the efficiency of their infrastructure. For example, in a large-scale financial services firm, vSphere can be used to consolidate hundreds of physical servers into a smaller number of ESXi hosts, reducing both the capital expenditure (CapEx) and operational expenditure (OpEx) of maintaining physical hardware.

In cloud environments, vSphere enables organizations to seamlessly integrate their on-premises infrastructure with public cloud services, creating hybrid clouds that offer greater flexibility and scalability. With features like vSphere Replication and Site Recovery Manager (SRM), businesses can implement robust disaster recovery solutions that minimize downtime and data loss in case of system failures.

PS

VMware vSphere 8.x continues to be a leading platform for virtualizing enterprise data centers and cloud environments. By enabling the efficient use of physical resources, improving system performance, and supporting both traditional and cloud-native applications, vSphere is essential for organizations looking to modernize their IT infrastructure. The introduction of the Distributed Services Engine and enhanced Kubernetes support solidifies vSphere's position as the backbone of modern data centers, helping businesses optimize their operations and reduce costs.

As businesses continue to evolve toward hybrid and multi-cloud architectures, VMware vSphere 8.x ensures that they have the flexibility, scalability, and performance needed to meet the demands of today's IT landscape.

IMPORTANCE OF VMWARE CERTIFICATIONS

Why VMware Certifications Matter

In the rapidly evolving world of information technology (IT), certifications have become a valuable asset for professionals looking to advance their careers. Among the most sought-after certifications are those offered by VMware, a leader in virtualization and cloud infrastructure technologies. VMware certifications validate an individual's ability to implement, manage, and troubleshoot VMware technologies, with the VMware vSphere 8.x Professional certification being one of the most relevant for IT professionals focusing on data center virtualization.

VMware certifications are recognized globally, setting the standard for skills in virtualization and cloud technologies. They offer a structured learning path for IT professionals, from foundational knowledge to expert-level proficiency, providing a benchmark that employers trust when hiring for technical roles. VMware certifications reflect not only the holder's technical expertise but also their commitment to staying current with industry advancements, making them highly valuable in a competitive job market.

Value for IT Professionals

Career Advancement Opportunities

VMware certifications open up new career opportunities for IT professionals by demonstrating expertise in virtualization and cloud infrastructure. Organizations around the world rely heavily on VMware technologies to power their data centers, and having certified professionals on staff ensures the smooth operation of these critical systems. As a result, certified VMware professionals are in high demand for roles such as systems administrators, network engineers, cloud architects, and virtualization specialists.

The VMware vSphere 8.x Professional certification is particularly important because vSphere is one of the most widely deployed virtualization platforms globally. Professionals certified in vSphere are equipped to manage complex virtual environments, a skill that is highly valued by enterprises looking to optimize their IT infrastructure. Additionally, this certification helps distinguish IT professionals from their peers, positioning them as experts in their field.

Higher Earning Potential

VMware certifications often lead to higher salaries, as they validate specialized skills that are critical to the management of IT infrastructure. According to surveys, professionals holding VMware certifications, such as the VMware Certified Professional (VCP), can command salaries significantly higher than those without certification. In some regions, certified VMware professionals earn up to 10-

15% more than their non-certified counterparts due to the critical nature of virtualization technologies in modern IT environments.

This increase in earning potential is a direct reflection of the value that businesses place on VMware-certified employees. As more organizations migrate to cloud environments and adopt hybrid IT infrastructures, the demand for professionals who can efficiently manage and optimize these environments continues to grow. VMware certifications ensure that IT professionals are equipped to meet these demands, making them a vital investment in career growth.

Enhanced Job Security

Virtualization has become a cornerstone of modern IT infrastructure, and VMware is a leading provider of virtualization solutions. As businesses move towards more scalable, efficient, and secure infrastructures, the reliance on VMware technologies increases. IT professionals who hold VMware certifications are often seen as indispensable assets, particularly in organizations where virtualized environments are central to business operations. Having a VMware certification, such as the vSphere 8.x Professional certification, enhances job security because certified professionals possess the necessary skills to ensure the stability and performance of these mission-critical environments.

Reflecting Industry Knowledge and Expertise

VMware certifications are more than just a credential—they are a testament to an individual's deep understanding of virtualization technologies and the ability to apply that knowledge in real-world scenarios. The certification process typically involves rigorous training and hands-on experience, ensuring that certified professionals are well-equipped to handle the complexities of VMware environments.

The vSphere 8.x Professional exam focuses on advanced topics such as virtual networking, storage management, high availability (HA), and disaster recovery, which are essential for managing a modern data center. These skills are crucial for maintaining business continuity, optimizing resource usage, and ensuring that IT services are delivered efficiently. By passing this certification exam, professionals demonstrate their ability to design, deploy, and manage VMware environments, aligning themselves with best practices and the latest industry standards.

Keeping Certifications Current with Technology Trends

Technology evolves rapidly, and IT professionals must stay up-to-date with the latest developments to remain competitive. VMware regularly updates its certifications to reflect the most current trends and advancements in its technology suite. The release of vSphere 8.x introduces new features such as the Distributed Services Engine (DPU), improved vSAN capabilities, and enhanced Kubernetes integration. These updates are crucial for organizations looking to modernize their infrastructures and support emerging technologies like containers and hybrid cloud deployments.

By pursuing and maintaining a VMware vSphere 8.x certification, professionals stay current with these advancements, ensuring they can implement and manage the latest features in VMware environments. This not only makes them more valuable to their current employers but also enhances their employability in a market where organizations are increasingly seeking to adopt cutting-edge technologies.

Keeping certifications up-to-date also signals a professional's commitment to continuous learning and development, which is a key trait that employers look for when hiring for technical roles. VMware's recertification policy, which encourages professionals to stay current with their certifications by passing new exams or upgrading their credentials, ensures that individuals maintain their expertise in an ever-changing IT landscape.

Relevance of vSphere 8.x Certification in Today's Virtualization Needs

The VMware vSphere 8.x Professional certification is particularly relevant in today's IT environment because of the increasing reliance on virtualization to drive efficiency, scalability, and cost savings. As more organizations embrace cloud computing, hybrid cloud architectures, and containerized applications, the skills validated by this certification become indispensable.

vSphere 8.x introduces enhanced capabilities that support both traditional and modern workloads, making it a versatile platform for businesses of all sizes. The certification ensures that IT professionals are well-versed in managing these environments, whether they are running legacy applications on virtual machines or deploying microservices using Kubernetes on vSphere with Tanzu.

PS

VMware certifications, especially the vSphere 8.x Professional certification, are a vital asset for IT professionals. They provide career growth opportunities, higher earning potential, and ensure that certified individuals remain at the forefront of technological advancements. As businesses continue to depend on virtualization and cloud solutions, these certifications will only become more valuable, making them a key investment for any IT professional looking to advance in their career.

KEY FEATURES IN VSPHERE 8.X

VMware vSphere 8.x introduces a suite of new features and enhancements designed to improve performance, scalability, and security within virtualized environments. These upgrades reflect the growing complexity of modern data centers and the need for a platform that supports both traditional and cloud-native applications. Key innovations in vSphere 8.x include the introduction of the Distributed Services Engine (DPU), significant vSAN enhancements, and improved Kubernetes integration through vSphere with Tanzu. These features position vSphere 8.x as a crucial platform for businesses looking to maximize the efficiency of their virtual infrastructure.

Distributed Services Engine (DPU)

One of the most groundbreaking features introduced in vSphere 8.x is the Distributed Services Engine, which leverages Data Processing Units (DPUs) to offload certain network and storage tasks from the CPU. The DPU, often referred to as a "SmartNIC," is a specialized hardware component that accelerates network and storage processing, freeing up CPU resources for other workloads.

How the DPU Works:

Traditionally, CPUs handle both compute tasks (running applications) and infrastructure tasks (like network and storage management). As data centers scale and workloads become more demanding, these infrastructure tasks can significantly impact overall performance, leading to inefficiencies. The Distributed Services Engine addresses this challenge by assigning network and storage tasks to the DPU, which is optimized for such workloads.

Performance Benefits: By offloading these tasks, the CPU can focus solely on application compute tasks, leading to better application performance and lower latency. This is particularly beneficial in environments with high data throughput and latency-sensitive applications, such as financial trading systems or real-time analytics.

Scalability Benefits: The DPU enables better resource utilization, allowing organizations to run more workloads on the same hardware. This feature is especially important in large-scale, cloud-native environments where compute resources are at a premium.

Security Improvements: The DPU also enhances security by isolating infrastructure tasks from the primary compute resources, reducing the attack surface for potential vulnerabilities. In multi-tenant environments, this isolation ensures that network and storage operations are secured at a hardware level, improving overall data security.

Real-World Use Case:

Consider a large financial services company handling thousands of transactions per second. In such an environment, low latency and high throughput are critical. By deploying DPUs in their vSphere 8.x environment, the company can ensure that networking and storage tasks are processed efficiently, minimizing latency and maximizing transaction speeds, while leaving CPUs free to focus on critical application processing.

vSAN Enhancements

vSphere 8.x brings several improvements to vSAN, VMware's software-defined storage solution that integrates with the hypervisor to pool direct-attached storage from ESXi hosts into a single, logical storage platform. The updates in vSphere 8.x make vSAN more efficient, scalable, and resilient.

Key Enhancements in vSAN 8.x:

Express Storage Architecture (ESA): One of the most significant updates in vSAN 8.x is the introduction of the Express Storage Architecture, which delivers improved performance and scalability for all-flash and hybrid configurations. This architecture simplifies storage operations, reduces overhead, and increases throughput, making it ideal for performance-intensive applications.

Improved Data Durability and Resiliency: vSAN 8.x introduces enhanced protection mechanisms for data, reducing the likelihood of data loss in the event of host failures. This includes faster recovery times for failed components and better fault tolerance across storage nodes.

Simplified Management: New management tools in vSAN 8.x improve the ease of monitoring and maintaining storage environments. Administrators benefit from automated health checks and intelligent insights that reduce the time spent troubleshooting storage issues.

Technical Benefits:

Performance: The new ESA in vSAN 8.x is designed to handle modern storage hardware more efficiently, leading to faster input/output operations per second (IOPS) and lower storage latencies. This makes it a preferred choice for organizations running high-performance databases or large-scale analytics applications.

Scalability: vSAN 8.x's architecture is built for scale, allowing businesses to expand their storage environments seamlessly as their data grows. This scalability is vital for organizations with evolving storage demands, such as those in healthcare or media production that manage large volumes of data.

Resiliency: Enhanced data durability in vSAN 8.x ensures that businesses can maintain uptime and avoid costly disruptions due to hardware failures. For industries that cannot afford downtime, such as e-commerce or healthcare, this level of resiliency is a significant advantage.

Real-World Use Case:

A healthcare provider dealing with massive amounts of patient data, including imaging and medical records, would benefit from the ESA in vSAN 8.x. The enhanced performance and storage scalability would allow the organization to manage their growing data needs while ensuring fast access to critical information, which is essential for patient care and compliance with healthcare regulations.

Kubernetes Integration with vSphere with Tanzu

vSphere with Tanzu in vSphere 8.x further enhances Kubernetes integration, making it easier for organizations to manage both virtual machines and containerized applications within a unified infrastructure. This integration is essential for businesses adopting DevOps practices and running cloud-native applications alongside traditional workloads.

Key Improvements:

Enhanced Kubernetes Control Plane: vSphere with Tanzu in vSphere 8.x offers a more streamlined Kubernetes control plane, making it easier to manage clusters, deploy workloads, and scale applications. This improves developer productivity and simplifies operations for IT administrators.

vSphere Zones: This new feature enables better workload management across data centers, allowing for geographically distributed deployments of Kubernetes clusters. It also enhances availability by ensuring that workloads can failover between zones seamlessly.

Improved Security: With vSphere 8.x, Kubernetes workloads are better integrated into the existing security policies of the vSphere environment. Administrators can enforce consistent security policies across both virtual machines and containers, ensuring that all workloads adhere to compliance requirements.

Technical Benefits:

Flexibility: By allowing organizations to run both VMs and containers on the same infrastructure, vSphere 8.x provides the flexibility needed to support hybrid application environments. This is particularly beneficial for businesses transitioning from traditional to cloud-native architectures.

Developer Agility: Developers can deploy and manage Kubernetes clusters directly through vSphere, enabling faster development cycles and reducing the operational burden on IT teams. This integration supports the agile methodologies that are common in modern software development environments.

Real-World Use Case:

A retail company looking to deploy a microservices architecture can use vSphere with Tanzu to manage its Kubernetes clusters while running existing legacy systems in VMs. The improved control plane and seamless integration with vSphere 8.x would allow the company to scale its microservices as demand increases, without overhauling its entire infrastructure.

PS

VMware vSphere 8.x introduces powerful features that cater to the performance, scalability, and security demands of modern IT environments. The Distributed Services Engine optimizes resource allocation by offloading tasks to DPUs, while the enhancements in vSAN ensure robust, scalable storage solutions. Additionally, vSphere with Tanzu improves Kubernetes integration, allowing organizations to manage both legacy and cloud-native applications efficiently. These innovations make vSphere 8.x an ideal platform for businesses looking to modernize their IT infrastructure and stay ahead in a competitive, data-driven world.

UNDERSTANDING VMWARE ESXI

VMware ESXi is a powerful, bare-metal hypervisor that forms the foundation of the VMware vSphere environment. It enables the virtualization of physical hardware by allowing multiple virtual machines (VMs) to run on a single server, each with its own operating system and applications. ESXi abstracts the underlying physical resources (CPU, memory, storage, and network) and allocates them dynamically to VMs based on the organization's needs.

ESXi is a critical component in modern IT infrastructures, offering a scalable, reliable, and efficient platform for hosting virtualized environments. Its ability to run independently of an underlying operating system, along with its compact architecture, makes it an ideal choice for enterprises aiming to optimize hardware usage, reduce costs, and improve system manageability.

Role of ESXi in the vSphere Environment

ESXi plays a pivotal role within the vSphere ecosystem, acting as the underlying hypervisor that allows businesses to virtualize their physical hardware and run multiple workloads on the same server. In vSphere, ESXi is responsible for handling the core virtualization tasks, including resource scheduling, VM isolation, and the distribution of physical resources to virtualized workloads.

The key responsibilities of VMware ESXi in a vSphere environment include

Abstraction of Physical Hardware: ESXi abstracts hardware resources like CPU, memory, storage, and networking, allowing VMs to use these resources without being aware of the underlying physical infrastructure.

Resource Allocation: ESXi dynamically allocates resources to VMs based on demand, ensuring that applications receive the necessary compute, memory, and storage resources to function optimally.

Workload Isolation: ESXi ensures that each VM is isolated from others on the same host, providing security and preventing conflicts between applications.

Efficient Resource Utilization: By enabling the use of multiple VMs on a single physical host, ESXi reduces the overall hardware footprint, leading to cost savings, better energy efficiency, and easier infrastructure management.

How ESXi Works as a Hypervisor

VMware ESXi is a Type 1 hypervisor, meaning it runs directly on the server hardware without needing an underlying operating system. This direct interaction with hardware allows ESXi to be highly efficient in terms of resource management and performance, with minimal overhead.

Here's a breakdown of how ESXi functions:

Hardware Layer: ESXi interacts directly with the hardware components of the server, including CPU, RAM, network adapters, and storage devices. It communicates with the hardware through device drivers, allowing it to access and control these resources.

VMKernel: The VMKernel is the core operating system of ESXi that handles key virtualization tasks, including memory management, CPU scheduling, and I/O operations. The VMKernel is lightweight and optimized for performance, allowing ESXi to run VMs with minimal overhead.

Virtual Machines: ESXi allows the creation of VMs, each of which runs its own operating system and applications. The VMKernel abstracts the hardware resources and presents them to the VMs as virtualized components (e.g., virtual CPUs, virtual memory, and virtual network adapters).

Installation of ESXi

The installation of VMware ESXi is straightforward and typically involves the following steps:

Hardware Preparation: Ensure that the server hardware meets VMware's compatibility requirements. This includes supported processors, sufficient RAM, and compatible storage devices.

Download the ESXi Image: Obtain the latest version of the ESXi image from VMware's website.

Boot from the Installation Media: Use a bootable USB drive, CD/DVD, or network boot to initiate the installation process.

Select Installation Options: The installation process will prompt you to select the target disk where ESXi will be installed. Typically, a local disk or flash drive is used.

Configure Network and Management Settings: After installation, configure basic settings such as the management IP address, hostname, and DNS settings.

Access the ESXi Management Interface: Once ESXi is installed and configured, access its management interface (the vSphere Client) through a web browser. From here, you can create VMs, manage resources, and configure advanced settings.

New Capabilities in ESXi 8.x

VMware ESXi 8.x brings several new features and enhancements that improve performance, security, and manageability. Some of the most notable advancements include:

Support for DPUs (Data Processing Units):

As part of the Distributed Services Engine in vSphere 8.x, ESXi can now offload network and storage tasks to DPUs, improving overall system performance by freeing up CPU resources for application workloads. This feature is especially beneficial for high-performance environments that require low latency and high throughput.

Improved Security Features:

ESXi 8.x introduces enhanced security features, such as support for vSphere Trust Authority, which ensures that only trusted hosts can access critical infrastructure resources. Additionally, VMware Secure Boot ensures that ESXi is booted with trusted firmware and software components, protecting against unauthorized changes.

Enhanced Hardware Compatibility:

ESXi 8.x expands support for the latest hardware, including NVMe devices, GPUs, and modern CPU architectures. This ensures that businesses can take full advantage of the latest advancements in server hardware to maximize performance and scalability.

vSphere Quick Boot:

This feature allows ESXi to bypass hardware initialization when rebooting, reducing downtime during system updates or patches. Quick Boot is especially useful in large data centers where minimizing downtime is critical.

Best Practices for Managing ESXi Hosts

Effective management of ESXi hosts ensures optimal performance, stability, and security in a virtualized environment. Here are some best practices:

Use vCenter Server for Centralized Management:

Although ESXi can be managed individually, it's best to use vCenter Server for centralized management of multiple hosts. vCenter provides advanced capabilities like Distributed Resource Scheduler (DRS), High Availability (HA), and vSphere Lifecycle Manager (vLCM) for easier patching and updates.

Enable Secure Boot and Lockdown Mode:

To enhance security, always enable Secure Boot and consider using Lockdown Mode, which restricts direct access to the ESXi host. This prevents unauthorized users from making changes directly to the host and improves compliance with security policies.

Regularly Monitor Host Health and Performance:

Use vCenter's Performance Monitoring tools to regularly check the resource usage of your ESXi hosts. Monitoring CPU, memory, and network performance can help identify potential bottlenecks or underutilized resources, allowing for proactive optimization.

Patch and Update ESXi Hosts Regularly:

Keeping ESXi hosts up to date is critical for security and performance. Use vSphere Lifecycle Manager to automate patching across your ESXi hosts, ensuring that they are running the latest updates and security fixes.

Troubleshooting Common ESXi Issues

Managing ESXi hosts often involves addressing common issues that may arise in the virtualized environment. Here are some common troubleshooting tips:

> **Network Connectivity Issues:** Ensure that the network adapters on the ESXi host are configured correctly and that proper VLANs are set up for network isolation. Check for misconfigurations in vSwitches and physical switches.
> **High CPU or Memory Usage:** Monitor resource usage and check for VMs that may be over-provisioned or misbehaving. Use DRS to automatically balance workloads across hosts to alleviate resource pressure.

Storage Latency Issues: Ensure that storage paths are configured correctly and that storage policies are optimized for the workloads. Use Storage I/O Control (SIOC) to prevent storage contention between VMs.

PS

VMware ESXi is the foundation of the vSphere platform, enabling organizations to virtualize their physical hardware and optimize the use of computing resources. With the release of vSphere 8.x, ESXi has become even more powerful, offering new capabilities like DPU support, enhanced security, and improved hardware compatibility. By following best practices for managing ESXi hosts and addressing common issues proactively, administrators can ensure a stable, secure, and efficient virtual infrastructure that meets the demands of modern IT environments.

Introduction to VMware vCenter Server

VMware vCenter Server is the central management hub of the vSphere environment, providing administrators with a comprehensive toolset to manage virtual infrastructures efficiently. It allows IT administrators to oversee and control all aspects of the vSphere environment, from provisioning virtual machines (VMs) to monitoring performance, managing resources, and ensuring the security and health of the entire infrastructure.

vCenter Server simplifies the management of complex virtual environments by offering a single interface for managing multiple ESXi hosts, virtual machines, storage, networking, and security. This centralized approach enhances visibility and control, allowing administrators to automate routine tasks and streamline the operational management of virtual infrastructures.

Primary Functions of vCenter Server

vCenter Server offers a wide range of functions designed to manage every aspect of a virtualized environment. The key features include:

Centralized Management

vCenter Server consolidates the management of multiple ESXi hosts into a single interface. Instead of managing each host individually, administrators can monitor, control, and configure all hosts and VMs through the vCenter interface. This centralized management is especially critical for large-scale environments where there are hundreds or even thousands of virtual machines spread across multiple data centers.

VM Provisioning

One of the primary functions of vCenter Server is to enable efficient VM provisioning. Through vCenter, administrators can quickly create, configure, and deploy new VMs. Templates can be used to standardize VM deployments, ensuring that each new VM is configured according to specific organizational policies. This simplifies the process of setting up new environments and reduces the risk of misconfigurations.

Performance Monitoring

Performance monitoring is a critical aspect of managing virtualized environments. vCenter Server provides built-in performance charts and reports that allow administrators to monitor key metrics such as CPU usage, memory utilization, disk I/O, and network traffic. These metrics help identify resource bottlenecks, optimize workloads, and ensure that virtual machines are operating efficiently.

vCenter's performance alarms and notifications allow administrators to set thresholds for different metrics, ensuring they are alerted when performance issues arise. This proactive monitoring helps prevent potential system failures or resource exhaustion.

vSphere High Availability (HA) and Fault Tolerance

vCenter Server enables High Availability (HA) across ESXi hosts, ensuring that virtual machines remain available even in the event of a host failure. When configured with HA, vCenter continuously monitors the health of ESXi hosts, and if one fails, it automatically restarts affected VMs on other available hosts. This feature is critical for maintaining business continuity in enterprise environments.

In addition, vSphere Fault Tolerance (FT) can be configured through vCenter Server. Fault Tolerance provides continuous availability by creating a live shadow instance of a VM on another host, ensuring that there is no downtime even in the event of a hardware failure.

vSphere Distributed Resource Scheduler (DRS)

DRS is a feature within vCenter Server that helps balance resources across a cluster of ESXi hosts. DRS automatically distributes VMs based on resource consumption, ensuring that no single host becomes overburdened while others remain underutilized. This automated load balancing enhances performance, reduces manual intervention, and ensures optimal resource utilization.

VM Snapshots and Cloning

vCenter Server simplifies the process of creating VM snapshots, which capture the state of a VM at a specific point in time. This allows administrators to easily revert to a previous state if needed, especially during testing, updates, or troubleshooting.

VM cloning is another feature available in vCenter, allowing for the duplication of VMs to quickly create new instances with identical configurations. This is particularly useful in test environments or when scaling services.

vCenter Server Appliance (VCSA) Installation and Configuration in vSphere 8.x

With the release of vSphere 8.x, the vCenter Server Appliance (VCSA) remains the preferred method for deploying vCenter. VCSA is a pre-packaged virtual machine that runs vCenter services on a Linux-based platform, replacing the older Windows-based vCenter installation. VCSA provides simplified management, easier updates, and enhanced performance compared to its predecessor.

Installation Process:

Download and Deploy the Appliance:

Administrators begin by downloading the vCenter Server Appliance ISO from the VMware website. The deployment process involves connecting to an ESXi host and launching the appliance installer.

Select Deployment Configuration:

During the installation process, administrators can choose the appropriate deployment size based on the number of hosts and VMs in the environment. For small environments, a basic setup with minimal resources may suffice, while larger environments may require a more robust configuration.

Configure Networking and Storage:

Administrators must specify the network settings for the VCSA, including IP address, gateway, and DNS information. Additionally, they need to configure the storage settings, specifying the datastore where the appliance's files will reside.

SSO (Single Sign-On) Configuration:

One of the critical steps during installation is configuring vCenter Single Sign-On (SSO). SSO allows administrators to manage multiple vCenter Servers using a single identity, simplifying authentication across environments.

Complete Installation:

Once the appliance is deployed, administrators can access the vSphere Client through a web browser and begin configuring and managing their environment.

Configuration in vSphere 8.x:

vCenter Server 8.x includes several new features that streamline lifecycle management and improve system performance:

Simplified Lifecycle Management:

vSphere 8.x introduces vSphere Lifecycle Manager (vLCM), which centralizes and simplifies the management of patches, updates, and firmware for both ESXi hosts and VCSA itself. With vLCM, administrators can apply consistent updates across multiple hosts and manage hardware compatibility checks, reducing the manual workload of maintaining a virtualized environment.

Improved Scalability and Performance:

vCenter Server in vSphere 8.x can support larger environments with more ESXi hosts and VMs, making it ideal for enterprises scaling up their infrastructure. Additionally, performance enhancements in the VCSA ensure faster response times and more efficient handling of large workloads.

Enhanced Security Features:

vCenter Server 8.x includes improvements in security, such as the integration with vSphere Trust Authority, which ensures that only trusted hosts can be added to the environment. Furthermore, VMware Secure Boot ensures that both ESXi hosts and VCSA boot securely, preventing unauthorized changes to the system.

Best Practices for Managing vCenter Server in Large-Scale Environments

In large-scale enterprise environments, managing vCenter Server effectively is crucial for maintaining system performance, security, and scalability. Here are some best practices:

Resource Planning:

Ensure that vCenter Server Appliance is provisioned with enough CPU, memory, and storage to handle the number of ESXi hosts and VMs in the environment. Under-provisioning can lead to performance degradation and delays in executing management tasks.

Regular Backups:

Implement regular backups of the vCenter Server Appliance to ensure rapid recovery in the event of a system failure. VMware offers vCenter Server Backup and Restore, which can be used to back up both the configuration and the database of the VCSA.

Enable Monitoring and Alerts:

Set up monitoring and performance alerts in vCenter Server to ensure timely responses to any issues that arise. Alarms can be configured for CPU, memory, storage, and network usage, as well as for more specific events like VM power state changes or host disconnections.

Use vSphere Tags and Custom Attributes:

For large environments, it's important to organize and categorize VMs, hosts, and storage efficiently. Using vSphere Tags and Custom Attributes helps administrators quickly filter and locate resources, improving the speed and efficiency of management tasks.

Patch and Update Regularly:

Use vLCM to ensure that ESXi hosts and VCSA are patched and updated regularly. Staying current with updates not only enhances performance but also ensures that the environment remains secure from vulnerabilities.

P.S.

VMware vCenter Server is the cornerstone of any vSphere deployment, offering centralized management and a host of features that simplify the administration of virtual environments. From VM provisioning to performance monitoring and high availability, vCenter Server provides the tools necessary to manage even the largest and most complex infrastructures. With the enhancements in vSphere 8.x, such as vLCM and improved security features, vCenter Server continues to be a critical component for organizations looking to optimize and scale their virtualized environments effectively.

New Distributed Services Engine (DPU)

The Distributed Services Engine (DPU) is one of the most significant innovations introduced in VMware vSphere 8.x, representing a shift in how compute, network, and storage tasks are managed in virtualized environments. This new feature leverages Data Processing Units (DPUs) to offload certain infrastructure tasks from the main CPU, providing significant improvements in performance, scalability, and security. DPUs, also referred to as SmartNICs, are specialized hardware components designed to handle specific network and storage functions more efficiently than general-purpose CPUs.

What are DPUs?

A DPU (Data Processing Unit) is a programmable hardware component that sits between the main CPU and the network interface. It is designed to offload tasks that would traditionally be processed by the CPU, such as network packet processing, storage I/O management, and security-related functions like encryption and firewalling. By offloading these infrastructure tasks, DPUs free up the CPU to focus on application workloads, improving overall system performance and efficiency.

The DPU typically consists of three main components:

A General-Purpose Processing Core (such as an ARM processor) that handles control plane operations.

Dedicated Hardware Accelerators for network and storage processing tasks, such as packet forwarding, encryption, or compression.

Programmable Software Modules that allow customization and flexibility for specific workloads and environments.

DPUs are particularly beneficial in modern data centers where workloads are highly dynamic, and performance demands are high. The introduction of DPUs in **vSphere 8.x** is part of VMware's broader effort to support cloud-native workloads and improve the efficiency of virtualization in environments that require low-latency and high-throughput network and storage processing.

Purpose of the Distributed Services Engine (DPU)

The primary purpose of the Distributed Services Engine is to enhance resource management by offloading network and storage infrastructure tasks from the CPU to the DPU. This results in several key benefits:

Improved CPU Efficiency: By offloading these tasks, the CPU can dedicate more of its resources to application processing, improving the overall performance of workloads. This is particularly important in environments running mission-critical applications or high-performance computing (HPC) workloads, where CPU cycles are often a limiting factor.

Enhanced Scalability: The DPU offloads essential network and storage functions, allowing for better scaling of applications without adding strain to the CPU. This is particularly advantageous in cloud-native environments where microservices and containerized applications often require rapid scaling of resources.

Better Isolation and Security: DPUs also improve security by providing hardware isolation between infrastructure tasks and application workloads. This isolation reduces the risk of interference or compromise between different layers of the system, offering a more secure environment for multi-tenant cloud platforms and hybrid environments.

Offloading Network and Storage Functions

In traditional environments, the CPU manages both compute (application workloads) and infrastructure tasks (networking, storage I/O, etc.). This architecture often leads to performance bottlenecks, especially when infrastructure tasks like packet forwarding, firewall enforcement, or encryption consume significant CPU resources.

The Distributed Services Engine addresses this challenge by offloading these infrastructure tasks to the DPU. Some of the critical network and storage functions that are typically offloaded include:

Network Packet Processing: DPUs handle the transmission and routing of network packets, reducing the CPU load associated with network traffic, especially in environments with high network throughput or complex routing requirements.

Firewall and Encryption: Many DPUs come with built-in hardware accelerators that handle encryption and firewall rules, enabling faster and more secure data transfers between virtual machines (VMs) and storage or network resources.

Storage I/O Management: The DPU also offloads storage-related tasks, such as handling input/output operations (I/O) between VMs and storage devices. This offloading is especially beneficial in storage-intensive environments like databases or data lakes, where high-volume storage operations can overwhelm the CPU.

Advantages of Using DPUs for Performance and Security

Performance Benefits

Increased CPU Headroom: One of the most significant advantages of the DPU is the increased CPU headroom available for application workloads. By offloading infrastructure tasks, vSphere 8.x ensures that more CPU resources are available to the VMs, improving the performance of applications, especially in environments with high compute requirements.

Lower Latency: DPUs provide lower latency for both network and storage operations, making them ideal for real-time applications that require fast data processing, such as financial services, high-frequency trading, or media streaming. The reduced CPU contention ensures that critical tasks can be processed without unnecessary delays.

Efficient Resource Utilization: With DPUs handling much of the infrastructure overhead, the remaining resources can be utilized more efficiently. This allows for greater VM density, meaning that more VMs can run on the same physical hardware without sacrificing performance.

Security Benefits

Isolation of Infrastructure Tasks: By isolating network and storage processing tasks from the CPU, DPUs create a hardware-enforced security barrier between infrastructure functions and user applications. This separation is crucial for maintaining the integrity of infrastructure operations in multi-tenant environments.

Enhanced Data Encryption: DPUs often include hardware-accelerated encryption, ensuring that data moving across the network or between storage devices is encrypted without compromising performance. This feature is particularly important for industries with stringent data security requirements, such as healthcare or government sectors.

Advanced Firewall Capabilities: With DPUs handling firewall enforcement at the hardware level, network traffic can be monitored and controlled more efficiently. This improves overall network security by preventing unauthorized traffic from reaching critical infrastructure resources.

Practical Use Cases for DPUs in Enterprise Environments

The Distributed Services Engine and DPUs provide significant advantages in various use cases, particularly in environments that require high performance, scalability, and security. Some practical applications include:

Cloud-Native Workloads

In cloud-native environments, where microservices and containers are deployed at scale, DPUs help to optimize resource utilization by offloading networking and storage tasks. This is particularly useful in Kubernetes clusters running on vSphere with Tanzu, where containerized workloads often require low-latency networking and rapid scaling of resources.

High-Performance Computing (HPC)

Organizations running HPC workloads, such as scientific simulations or large-scale data analysis, benefit from the increased CPU efficiency provided by DPUs. By offloading non-compute tasks, the CPU can focus solely on the application's heavy computational tasks, improving overall throughput and reducing processing times.

Multi-Tenant Cloud Platforms

In multi-tenant cloud environments, DPUs enhance security and isolation between tenants. By offloading network and security functions, cloud providers can ensure that each tenant's infrastructure tasks are processed independently of other tenants, reducing the risk of cross-tenant interference or security breaches.

Financial Services and Real-Time Analytics

Industries that rely on real-time data processing, such as financial services, can take advantage of DPUs to reduce latency and improve throughput. For example, high-frequency trading platforms require extremely low-latency network connections to process trades in milliseconds, making DPUs an ideal solution for ensuring fast and secure data transfer.

Preparing for Exam Questions on DPUs

When preparing for the VMware vSphere 8.x Professional exam, it's important to focus on the role of DPUs and the Distributed Services Engine. Exam questions may cover the following topics:

Understanding DPU architecture and how it interacts with ESXi hosts and virtualized environments.

Use cases for DPUs in modern, cloud-native, and high-performance environments.

Security advantages provided by offloading tasks to DPUs, including encryption and network isolation.

Performance improvements achieved through offloading network and storage tasks from the CPU to the DPU.

Being familiar with these concepts will help candidates confidently answer questions related to VMware vSphere 8.x's Distributed Services Engine and its implementation in enterprise environments.

vSphere Networking Overview

vSphere networking is a critical component of VMware's virtualization platform, enabling communication between virtual machines (VMs), physical networks, and other vSphere infrastructure components. By providing a robust, scalable, and flexible networking model, vSphere supports high-performance environments where multiple workloads and services coexist. VMware vSphere offers various tools for managing virtual networking, including virtual switches (vSwitches), distributed switches, VLANs, and Network I/O Control (NIOC). These components work together to create highly available, secure, and efficient network infrastructures.

Virtual Switches (vSwitch)

A virtual switch (vSwitch) is a software-based network switch that allows VMs running on the same ESXi host to communicate with each other, as well as with external networks. Similar to physical network switches, a vSwitch manages the flow of data between virtual network interfaces (vNICs) assigned to VMs and the physical network interfaces (pNICs) of the ESXi host.

vSphere offers two types of virtual switches:

Standard vSwitch (vSS): A Standard vSwitch operates at the host level, providing basic network connectivity for VMs. Each ESXi host requires its own configuration of vSS, which is managed individually. Standard switches are ideal for smaller environments or cases where each host is managed separately.

Distributed vSwitch (vDS): A vSphere Distributed Switch (vDS) provides centralized management of networking across multiple ESXi hosts, offering more advanced features like port mirroring, load balancing, and better monitoring capabilities. A vDS enables consistent network configurations across a cluster, improving efficiency in large-scale environments. Instead of configuring network settings on each host, administrators can configure the vDS once through vCenter Server, and the configuration is automatically applied to all hosts within the cluster.

VLANs (Virtual Local Area Networks)

Virtual Local Area Networks (VLANs) play an essential role in vSphere networking by enabling the logical segmentation of a network into multiple virtual networks. VLANs are used to isolate traffic, improve security, and reduce broadcast domain sizes within the network.

VLAN Configuration: In a vSphere environment, VLANs are typically implemented by tagging traffic with VLAN IDs using the IEEE 802.1Q standard. Each VLAN is assigned a unique VLAN ID, which is used to segregate traffic. VLANs allow network administrators to group VMs into separate logical networks, even if they are running on the same physical host or network segment.

Use Case for VLANs: A common use case for VLANs in vSphere networking is to separate different types of traffic, such as management traffic, storage traffic, vMotion traffic, and production traffic. This segmentation improves security and ensures that sensitive data, such as management traffic, is isolated from other network traffic.

Example of VLAN Setup: If you want to isolate VM traffic for different departments in an organization (e.g., finance and HR), you would:

1. Create separate VLANs for each department.
2. Assign VLAN IDs (e.g., VLAN 100 for Finance, VLAN 200 for HR).
3. Configure the vSwitch or Vds to map VM network adapters to the appropriate VLANs based on these IDs.

P.S.

In this configuration, VMs in the finance department can only communicate with other VMs in the same VLAN unless specific routing or firewall rules are configured to allow cross-VLAN traffic.

Network I/O Control (NIOC)

Network I/O Control (NIOC) is a feature that allows administrators to prioritize network traffic types and allocate bandwidth on distributed switches. In a multi-tenant or high-traffic environment, NIOC ensures that critical traffic, such as vMotion or management traffic, has guaranteed access to network resources, preventing non-essential traffic from consuming excessive bandwidth.

NIOC Traffic Types: NIOC categorizes traffic into several classes, such as vMotion, management, VM traffic, and fault tolerance. Each traffic type can be assigned a specific bandwidth limit or share, allowing administrators to control the network's behavior under congestion. For example, you might want to ensure that vMotion traffic, which can be bandwidth-intensive, doesn't interfere with production VM traffic.

Dynamic Resource Allocation: NIOC dynamically adjusts bandwidth allocation based on the real-time needs of each traffic type. This ensures that even during periods of high network utilization, critical traffic has sufficient bandwidth to maintain performance and availability. NIOC is particularly useful in environments with diverse workloads, where some traffic types (such as storage or vMotion) might temporarily require more bandwidth than others.

Example of NIOC Configuration: In a vSphere environment, if you want to ensure that management traffic always has at least 30% of available bandwidth, you can configure NIOC to allocate 30% of the distributed switch's bandwidth for this traffic type. This prevents scenarios where heavy VM traffic might starve the management network, causing potential issues in managing the ESXi hosts or VMs.

Best Practices for Setting Up vSphere Networking

Implementing a well-designed network architecture is critical for maintaining high availability, performance, and security in a vSphere environment. Here are some best practices for configuring vSphere networking:

Use Distributed Switches for Centralized Management: For large-scale environments with multiple ESXi hosts, always use vSphere Distributed Switches (vDS) over Standard vSwitches. vDS simplifies network management by centralizing configurations and ensuring consistency across hosts. It also enables advanced features such as Network I/O Control (NIOC), NetFlow, and port mirroring.

Separate Network Traffic with VLANs: Implement VLANs to segregate different types of network traffic. For example, create VLANs for management, storage, vMotion, and VM traffic to isolate these networks and improve security. This also helps in reducing the broadcast domain size and network congestion.

Enable NIOC for Traffic Prioritization: In environments where multiple types of traffic share the same physical NICs (e.g., management, storage, vMotion), use Network I/O Control (NIOC) to prioritize traffic based on the organization's needs. This ensures that critical traffic, such as management or fault tolerance traffic, always has access to sufficient bandwidth, even during times of high network congestion.

Utilize Redundant Uplinks: Always configure multiple uplinks (pNICs) for vSwitches and vDS to provide redundancy and ensure network availability. In case one physical NIC fails, traffic can be automatically rerouted through the remaining uplinks, maintaining network connectivity for VMs and vSphere services.

Monitor and Optimize Network Performance: Regularly monitor network performance using vSphere's built-in tools such as vRealize Operations or third-party solutions. Pay attention to key metrics like latency, throughput, and packet loss to identify and resolve potential bottlenecks before they impact performance.

Use Jumbo Frames for Storage and vMotion Traffic: When dealing with high-bandwidth traffic, such as storage or vMotion, enable Jumbo Frames (frames larger than 1500 bytes) to reduce overhead and increase throughput. This is particularly useful in iSCSI or vMotion configurations, where reducing network packet size can significantly improve performance.

P.S.

By applying these best practices, organizations can ensure that their vSphere networking infrastructure is highly available, secure, and capable of supporting high-performance workloads. This combination of vSwitches, distributed switches, VLANs, and NIOC creates a resilient and efficient network architecture, capable of handling the complex demands of modern virtualized environments.

INSTALLING VMWARE ESXI

Overview of VMware ESXi Installation

VMware ESXi is a bare-metal hypervisor that enables businesses to virtualize their physical servers and run multiple virtual machines (VMs) on a single piece of hardware. As part of the vSphere ecosystem, ESXi plays a crucial role in server virtualization, providing the foundation for building efficient and scalable IT infrastructures. In VMware vSphere 8.x, ESXi introduces several new features and improvements to further optimize performance and security. Installing ESXi 8.x involves meeting hardware requirements, following a step-by-step installation process, and performing essential post-installation configurations to prepare the system for production use.

Hardware Requirements for ESXi 8.x

Before installing VMware ESXi 8.x, it's essential to ensure that the server hardware meets VMware's compatibility and performance requirements. Failing to meet these requirements can result in poor performance or incompatibility issues.

Minimum Hardware Requirements:

Processor (CPU):
- A 64-bit x86 processor with a minimum of 2 cores.
- Support for Intel VT-x or AMD-V (hardware virtualization extensions) and 64-bit guest operating systems.
- Support for Intel EM64T or AMD64 processors.

Memory (RAM):

Minimum of 4 GB of RAM; however, for optimal performance, it is recommended to have at least 8 GB or more, depending on the number of VMs you plan to run.

Storage:

- At least 32 GB of local storage for installing ESXi.
- SSD storage is recommended for improved performance.

P.S.

Ensure that the storage controller is supported by VMware; use the VMware Compatibility Guide to confirm hardware compatibility.

Network:

- At least one physical NIC supported by VMware.
- Gigabit Ethernet or higher is recommended for networking performance.

BIOS Settings:

- Ensure that Intel VT-x or AMD-V virtualization features are enabled in the BIOS.
- Enable Intel VT-d or AMD IOMMU for improved I/O performance.

Checking Compatibility:

Before proceeding with the installation, verify that your hardware (especially storage controllers and NICs) is compatible with VMware ESXi 8.x by referring to the VMware Hardware Compatibility Guide (HCG). This ensures that the system is supported, and all drivers required for optimal performance are available.

Steps for Installing VMware ESXi 8.x

Once the hardware requirements are met, you can begin the installation process for ESXi 8.x. The installation steps are straightforward, and VMware provides a user-friendly installer interface.

Step 1: Prepare the Installation Media

- Download the ESXi 8.x ISO:
- Go to the VMware Customer Connect portal and download the latest version of the ESXi 8.x ISO image.
- Ensure you select the version that matches your hardware (custom ISO images may be required for vendor-specific drivers).
- Create a Bootable USB Drive:
- Use a tool like Rufus or UNetbootin to create a bootable USB drive with the ESXi ISO image. Alternatively, you can burn the ISO to a CD/DVD if the server supports optical media.

Step 2: Boot from the Installation Media

- Insert the Bootable USB or CD/DVD:
- Insert the installation media into the physical server or virtual machine where you plan to install ESXi.
- Access the BIOS/Boot Menu:
- Restart the server and access the BIOS or Boot Menu by pressing the appropriate key (e.g., F12, Esc, or Del).
- Select the USB or CD/DVD drive as the boot device.
- Launch the VMware ESXi Installer:

The system will boot into the VMware ESXi Installer screen. Select "Install VMware ESXi 8.x" to begin the installation process.

Step 3: Install VMware ESXi 8.x

- Accept the End User License Agreement (EULA):
- Read and accept the VMware End User License Agreement (EULA) to proceed with the installation.
- Select the Installation Disk:

The installer will scan for available storage devices. Choose the disk where you want to install ESXi.

It's recommended to install ESXi on a dedicated SSD or HDD, separate from data storage drives to ensure better performance.

Configure Keyboard Layout:

- Select the keyboard layout that matches your region or preference.
- Set the Root Password:
- Enter a strong password for the root account. The root account has full administrative privileges, so ensure the password is secure and difficult to guess.
- Start the Installation:
- Once the disk and password are configured, the installer will begin copying files and installing ESXi. This process typically takes only a few minutes.
- Reboot the Server:

After installation is complete, the system will prompt you to reboot the server. Remove the installation media to prevent booting from the USB drive or CD/DVD again.

Step 4: Post-Installation Configuration

After the ESXi installation is complete and the server reboots, you will need to perform some basic configuration to get the host ready for production use.

Configure Management Network (DCUI):

- Upon reboot, the Direct Console User Interface (DCUI) will appear on the screen. This interface allows you to configure the network settings for managing the ESXi host.
- Press F2 to log in using the root account and configure the Management Network.
- Set the IP address, subnet mask, and gateway for the management interface. Assigning a static IP address is recommended for stability.

Configure DNS and Hostname:

In the DCUI, configure the DNS settings and assign a hostname to the ESXi host. This ensures the host can be identified in the network and resolve domain names properly.

Test Network Connectivity:

After configuring the network, use the ping test in the DCUI to verify that the ESXi host can communicate with other devices in the network (e.g., your management workstation or vCenter Server).

Connect to the vSphere Client:

- Once the network is configured, you can manage the ESXi host using the vSphere Client. Open a web browser and enter the management IP address (e.g., https://<IP_Address>/ui).
- Log in using the root credentials to access the host's management interface.
- Optimizing Performance and Security

Performance Optimization Tips:

Enable Hyper-Threading:

If your server's CPU supports hyper-threading, enable it in the BIOS to improve performance for workloads that benefit from multi-threading.

Use SSDs for Datastores:

Whenever possible, use solid-state drives (SSDs) for creating datastores. SSDs offer faster read/write speeds and lower latency compared to traditional hard disk drives (HDDs), improving VM performance.

Configure Jumbo Frames:

If you're using iSCSI or NFS storage, configure Jumbo Frames in your network settings. Jumbo Frames allow larger packets to be transmitted, reducing CPU overhead and improving network throughput.

Security Optimization Tips:

Enable Secure Boot:

Secure Boot ensures that only signed and trusted software is loaded during the boot process. It helps prevent unauthorized changes to the hypervisor and ensures the integrity of the ESXi host.

Enable Lockdown Mode:

For enhanced security, especially in production environments, enable Lockdown Mode on ESXi. Lockdown Mode prevents users from accessing the ESXi host directly through SSH or the DCUI, ensuring that all management actions are performed through vCenter Server.

Use Strong Password Policies:

Enforce strong password policies for all user accounts, especially the root account. Consider using two-factor authentication (2FA) for enhanced security in environments with high-security requirements.

Install Security Patches Regularly:

VMware frequently releases security patches and updates for ESXi. Use vSphere Lifecycle Manager (vLCM) to automate the deployment of patches and updates, ensuring that your hosts are protected against known vulnerabilities.

Common Challenges and Solutions

Driver Compatibility Issues:

If you encounter issues where ESXi does not detect storage controllers or network adapters, check the VMware Compatibility Guide to ensure that you're using supported drivers. You may need to download custom ESXi images provided by hardware vendors that include the necessary drivers.

Failed Installation Due to Incompatible Hardware:

If the installation fails because the hardware is not compatible, double-check the BIOS settings for virtualization technology (Intel VT-x/AMD-V) and hardware compatibility. Ensure all necessary hardware features are enabled.

Network Connectivity Issues:

After installation, if you cannot connect to the ESXi host through the network, verify that the correct IP address, subnet mask, and gateway are configured. Check network cabling and switch port configurations to ensure proper network connectivity.

Deploying vCenter Server Appliance (VCSA)

The vCenter Server Appliance (VCSA) is a preconfigured, Linux-based virtual machine optimized to run VMware vCenter Server services, providing a streamlined and efficient solution for managing vSphere environments. In vSphere 8.x, VCSA remains the preferred method of deploying vCenter Server, offering improved scalability, performance, and simplified lifecycle management. This section covers the deployment and configuration of VCSA, including essential steps like Single Sign-On (SSO) setup and integrating VCSA with ESXi hosts. We'll also discuss best practices for managing a vSphere environment with VCSA, focusing on backup and recovery strategies.

Steps to Install vCenter Server Appliance (VCSA)

1. Download the VCSA Installer

- Visit the VMware Customer Connect portal and download the vCenter Server Appliance 8.x ISO file. This ISO contains the installer for VCSA, along with necessary deployment tools.

2. Mount the ISO and Launch the Installer

- After downloading, mount the ISO on your local machine or server and navigate to the installer directory.
- Run the installer executable and select the Deploy vCenter Server Appliance option. The installer provides an easy-to-use GUI for deploying VCSA.

3. Select Deployment Type

Choose between deploying a vCenter Server with an Embedded Platform Services Controller (PSC) or External PSC. For most use cases, VMware recommends deploying the embedded configuration, which integrates all services (vCenter and PSC) into a single appliance, simplifying management and reducing overhead.

4. Connect to the ESXi Host

Provide the ESXi host credentials where VCSA will be deployed. The VCSA installer requires access to the ESXi host to deploy the appliance as a virtual machine.

5. Configure VCSA Settings

- VM Name: Specify a name for the vCenter Server Appliance.
- Size Selection: Choose the appropriate deployment size based on the number of hosts and VMs in your environment. VMware provides deployment size recommendations ranging from Tiny (up to 10 hosts) to X-Large (up to 2,000 hosts). It's essential to select the correct size to ensure optimal performance.
- Storage Configuration: Select the datastore on which VCSA will be deployed. Ensure that the datastore has adequate space, and consider using SSD storage for better performance.

6. Network Configuration

- Configure the network settings for VCSA, including the hostname, IP address, subnet mask, and gateway. Assigning a static IP address is recommended for stability and ease of management.
- Ensure that DNS is correctly configured, as vCenter Server relies heavily on DNS for communication within the vSphere environment.

7. Single Sign-On (SSO) Configuration

- Set up vCenter Single Sign-On (SSO). SSO is an authentication service that allows users to log in to vSphere components (vCenter, ESXi, etc.) with a single set of credentials. During installation, you'll either:
- Create a new SSO domain: This is required for the first deployment in a new vSphere environment. You will specify the SSO domain name (default is vsphere.local) and the administrator password.
- Join an existing SSO domain: If you're adding VCSA to an existing vSphere environment with an established SSO domain, provide the credentials to join the domain.
- Configuring SSO ensures secure and simplified access to vSphere components, eliminating the need for multiple logins and streamlining user management.

8. Start the Deployment

- After configuring the above settings, initiate the deployment process. The installer will upload the VCSA image to the selected ESXi host, power it on, and begin the configuration.
- Once the deployment is complete, the VCSA will be accessible through a web browser. Administrators can manage vCenter through the vSphere Client by navigating to the VCSA IP address or hostname (e.g., https://<vcsa-IP>/ui).

Integrating VCSA with ESXi Hosts

After deploying VCSA, the next step is to add ESXi hosts to the vCenter Server environment. This integration allows vCenter Server to manage the configuration, resource allocation, and monitoring of the ESXi hosts and VMs running on them.

1. Log in to vSphere Client

- Open a web browser and connect to the VCSA management interface (https://<vcsa-IP>/ui).
- Log in using the SSO administrator account you created during the installation process.

2. Add ESXi Hosts

- In the vSphere Client, navigate to Hosts and Clusters.
- Right-click the Datacenter object or a specific folder and select Add Host.
- Enter the FQDN or IP address of the ESXi host you want to add, and provide the host credentials.

3. Configure Host Settings

- The vCenter Server will validate the connection to the ESXi host. Once validated, you can configure additional settings such as resource pools, datastores, and networking.
- After adding the host, it will appear in the Hosts and Clusters view, and you can begin managing VMs, networks, and storage associated with that host.

Best Practices for Managing vSphere with VCSA

Effective management of a vSphere environment requires following best practices to ensure performance, security, and reliability. Below are some key considerations for managing VCSA in production environments:

1. Backup and Recovery of VCSA

VCSA is critical to the functioning of the vSphere environment, making regular backups essential to protect against data loss or system failure. VMware offers built-in tools to back up the VCSA configuration and database:

File-Based Backup: Use the vCenter Server Management Interface (VAMI) to configure file-based backups of VCSA. Backups can be scheduled to occur regularly, and you can store the backup files on remote servers using protocols like FTP, SCP, or NFS. These backups include the VCSA configuration, inventory data, and database contents.

vSphere Replication: For added redundancy, you can use vSphere Replication to replicate the vCenter Server Appliance to a secondary site, ensuring disaster recovery capabilities in the event of a site failure.

When restoring VCSA, use the VCSA restore tool, which can restore the configuration and data from a backup, minimizing downtime.

2. Monitor Resource Usage

Regularly monitor the resource usage of VCSA, especially in larger environments where the number of ESXi hosts and VMs can grow significantly. Keep an eye on CPU, memory, and storage usage to ensure the appliance has sufficient resources to perform optimally. If necessary, adjust the VCSA virtual machine's resource allocation through vSphere Client.

3. Apply Security Patches and Updates

VMware frequently releases updates and patches for vCenter Server to address security vulnerabilities and improve stability. Use vSphere Lifecycle Manager (vLCM) to automate the patching process for VCSA and ensure it remains up to date. This approach reduces the risk of security breaches and improves system reliability.

4. Enable Monitoring and Alerts

Configure monitoring and alerting for critical vSphere components using vCenter alarms. Set thresholds for CPU, memory, storage usage, and network performance to detect and respond to performance degradation or system failures promptly. Alarms can notify administrators via email or SNMP when issues arise, allowing for proactive maintenance and faster troubleshooting.

5. Schedule Regular Maintenance Tasks

Periodically perform maintenance tasks such as database cleanup, log rotation, and resource rebalancing to keep VCSA operating efficiently. vCenter Server Tasks can be scheduled to automate repetitive tasks, such as VM snapshots, host maintenance, or inventory management. Automating these tasks frees up administrative time and reduces the potential for human error.

By following these best practices, administrators can ensure a stable, secure, and scalable vSphere environment while maintaining operational efficiency and minimizing downtime.

Configuring vSphere Networking (vSwitches, VLANs)

VMware vSphere 8.x provides powerful networking capabilities that allow administrators to create and manage virtual networks in their virtualized environments. Networking in vSphere is crucial for enabling communication between virtual machines (VMs), physical networks, and storage. The two main types of network switches in vSphere are Standard Switches (vSwitches) and Distributed Switches (vDS). These switches enable you to connect VMs to each other and to the outside world while managing network traffic efficiently. Another important aspect of vSphere networking is VLANs (Virtual Local Area Networks), which allow administrators to segment network traffic for better security and performance.

<u>Standard Switches (vSwitch)</u>

A Standard vSwitch is a software-based virtual switch that runs locally on each ESXi host. It functions similarly to a physical network switch, forwarding traffic between VMs on the same host and between VMs and the physical network via the host's physical NICs (pNICs). Each ESXi host can have multiple standard switches, but each switch is configured and managed individually per host.

Key Features of Standard Switches:

Local Management: A vSwitch is configured on each ESXi host, and its settings apply only to that host. To configure networking across multiple hosts, administrators need to manually configure each switch individually.

Basic Features: Standard vSwitches provide basic Layer 2 networking features, including support for VLANs, port groups, NIC teaming, and traffic shaping.

Simpler Configuration: Standard switches are ideal for smaller environments where each host can be managed individually, or for testing environments where the overhead of a distributed switch is not required.

Configuration Example for a Standard Switch:

Create a vSwitch: In the vSphere Client, navigate to the Networking tab, right-click the ESXi host, and select Add Networking. Choose Virtual Machine Port Group for a Standard Switch.

Assign NICs: Select the physical NICs (pNICs) that will be used for the switch uplinks.

Create Port Groups: Define port groups for the VMs. Port groups allow for logical segmentation of traffic. You can associate each port group with different VLANs, if needed.

Set VLAN ID: When creating the port group, assign a VLAN ID to enable network segmentation and ensure traffic is tagged and routed correctly.

When to Use Standard Switches:

- Use Standard Switches (vSwitches) in smaller or isolated environments where each host is managed independently.
- They are also suitable for lab or testing environments where advanced networking features (e.g., traffic mirroring, centralized management) are not necessary.

Distributed Switches (vDS)

A vSphere Distributed Switch (vDS) is an advanced virtual switch that spans multiple ESXi hosts, offering centralized management of networking settings and advanced features not available in standard switches. A vDS enables a single configuration to be applied to multiple hosts, reducing the overhead of managing network settings across hosts individually.

Key Features of Distributed Switches:

Centralized Management: With a vDS, network configuration is managed through vCenter Server, allowing network settings to be applied uniformly across all hosts connected to the vDS. This is particularly useful in large-scale environments with many hosts.

Advanced Networking Features: Distributed switches offer advanced features like Network I/O Control (NIOC), NetFlow, port mirroring, and load balancing based on resource usage. These features provide better control and visibility of network traffic.

Improved Scalability: A vDS is designed for environments with large numbers of hosts and VMs, simplifying network management and reducing configuration errors.

Configuration Example for a Distributed Switch:

Create a vDS: In the vSphere Client, navigate to Networking and right-click on the Datacenter or Cluster. Select New Distributed Switch.

Select ESXi Hosts: Choose the ESXi hosts that will be added to the distributed switch.

Add Uplink Ports: Assign physical NICs (pNICs) from the hosts to act as uplinks for the vDS. These uplinks provide network connectivity between the virtual and physical networks.

Create Port Groups: As with a standard switch, create port groups and assign VLANs for network segmentation. However, with a vDS, these port groups are consistent across all hosts connected to the switch, ensuring uniform traffic management.

When to Use Distributed Switches:

- Use Distributed Switches (vDS) in larger environments where multiple ESXi hosts need to share a consistent network configuration. vDS is also suitable when advanced networking features like Network I/O Control (NIOC) or NetFlow are required.
- VLANs (Virtual Local Area Networks)
- VLANs are a crucial part of virtual networking, allowing administrators to segment network traffic logically. This segmentation can improve both security and performance by isolating different types of traffic (e.g., separating production traffic from management traffic).

How VLANs Work in vSphere:

VLANs are identified by VLAN IDs, which are tagged to network packets using the IEEE 802.1Q standard. When VMs send traffic through a virtual switch, the traffic is tagged with the appropriate VLAN ID. This ensures that only traffic destined for a specific VLAN is received by VMs or physical devices on that VLAN.

VLANs are configured within port groups on both standard switches and distributed switches. When configuring a port group, you specify the VLAN ID to which the port group is associated.

Example of VLAN Configuration:

Standard Switch VLAN Configuration: When creating a port group on a standard switch, assign a VLAN ID in the VLAN ID field (e.g., VLAN 100 for management traffic).

Distributed Switch VLAN Configuration: Similarly, on a vDS, assign VLAN IDs to port groups that span across multiple hosts. This ensures that traffic between VMs on different hosts remains isolated within the same VLAN.

When to Use VLANs:

- Use VLANs to isolate different types of traffic, such as management, storage, vMotion, or VM traffic.
- VLANs are critical in multi-tenant environments or scenarios where security policies require network segmentation (e.g., isolating traffic for different departments in an organization).

Key Differences Between vSwitches and vDS

Feature	Standard Switch (vSwitch)	Distributed Switch (vDS)
Management	Local to each ESXi host	Centralized management via vCenter
Scope	Host-level only	Across multiple hosts
Advanced Features	Basic Layer 2 functionality	Advanced features like NIOC, NetFlow
Port Group Consistency	Configured per host	Consistent across all hosts
Use Case	Small or isolated environments	Large, multi-host environments

EXAM CONSIDERATIONS

For the VMware vSphere 8.x Professional certification, networking concepts such as vSwitches, Distributed Switches, and VLANs are essential. Expect exam questions to focus on the differences between vSwitches and vDS, when to use each type of switch, and how VLANs are configured to ensure secure and segmented network traffic. Specific scenarios may test your ability to configure and troubleshoot network settings in both standard and distributed switches, as well as your knowledge of advanced features like Network I/O Control (NIOC). Additionally, the exam may cover how to ensure network redundancy and fault tolerance by configuring multiple uplinks or using VLANs for high availability.

P.S

By mastering these concepts, you'll be well-prepared to handle vSphere networking both in real-world environments and during the certification exam.

Regular practice in a lab environment with both vSwitch and vDS configurations can greatly help in understanding and troubleshooting common networking issues in vSphere.

RESOURCE POOLS AND RESOURCE ALLOCATION IN VMWARE VSPHERE 8.X

Purpose of Resource Pools

In VMware vSphere 8.x, resource pools serve as logical containers within an ESXi host or cluster, designed to allocate and manage compute resources such as CPU, memory, and storage among multiple virtual machines (VMs) or groups of VMs. Resource pools allow administrators to partition available physical resources into smaller, manageable segments, making it easier to allocate resources according to business needs or organizational units. By grouping VMs within resource pools, administrators can ensure that different applications or departments receive a fair share of resources, all while maintaining flexibility to adapt to changing demands.

Key benefits of using resource pools include:

Hierarchical Resource Management: Resource pools can be nested to create a hierarchy that reflects organizational structures or application groupings. This allows for more granular control over resource allocation.

Isolation and Containment: Resource pools can limit the impact of resource contention. For example, a misbehaving or resource-hungry VM within a resource pool will not affect other resource pools or VMs outside of that pool.

Scalability: Resource pools can grow or shrink dynamically based on the available resources and can easily be adjusted as business requirements change.

Creating and Managing Resource Pools

Creating a Resource Pool

To create a resource pool in vSphere 8.x, follow these steps:

1. **Access the vSphere Client:** Log in to the vSphere Client using your vCenter Server credentials.
2. **Navigate to the Host or Cluster:** In the Hosts and Clusters view, select the ESXi host or cluster where you want to create the resource pool.
3. **Create the Resource Pool:** Right-click the host or cluster and choose New Resource Pool. This opens a dialog where you can configure the name, CPU, and memory settings for the pool.

a. **Configure CPU and Memory Shares, Limits, and Reservations:**
   - **Shares:** Allocate relative priority for CPU and memory resources among multiple resource pools or VMs. Shares determine how resources are distributed when there is contention.
   - **Limits:** Set an upper limit on the CPU or memory that a resource pool can consume. This ensures that the resource pool does not consume more than the specified amount, even if additional resources are available.
   - **Reservations:** Specify the minimum guaranteed amount of CPU or memory resources for the resource pool. These resources are reserved for the pool, ensuring they are available even during periods of high contention.
4. **Save and Apply Settings:** Once the resource pool is configured, click OK to create it.

Managing Resource Pools

After creation, resource pools can be managed using the vSphere Client. Administrators can:

1. **Modify Shares, Limits, and Reservations:** As resource demands change, administrators can adjust the resource settings to ensure that each pool gets the appropriate resources.
2. **Add VMs or Nested Resource Pools:** Administrators can assign VMs or create nested resource pools within existing resource pools. This creates a hierarchical structure, allowing for fine-tuned resource control.
3. **Monitor Resource Usage:** The Resource Allocation tab in the vSphere Client provides insights into how CPU, memory, and storage resources are being used by VMs and resource pools. Administrators can monitor resource usage and adjust settings as needed to optimize performance.

Resource Pool Example

Consider a scenario where an organization has three departments—Finance, HR, and IT—each with its own VMs running critical applications. By creating a resource pool for each department, the administrator can allocate resources based on each department's needs:

- The Finance resource pool may have higher CPU and memory reservations since it runs CPU-intensive financial applications.
- The HR resource pool may have medium priority for resources, with a moderate reservation for its HR systems.
- The IT resource pool might be allocated fewer resources, but its VMs can still share unused capacity from other pools.

Resource Allocation in VMware vSphere

Resource allocation in vSphere refers to the distribution of compute resources—primarily CPU, memory, and storage—among VMs or resource pools. Proper resource allocation ensures that critical applications receive the necessary resources while maintaining overall system stability and performance.

CPU Allocation

CPU allocation in vSphere is managed using shares, reservations, and limits:

Shares: Represent a relative value used to allocate CPU resources among VMs or resource pools during contention. A VM with more shares receives more CPU resources than one with fewer shares when the ESXi host is under heavy load.

Reservations: Specify the minimum amount of CPU that a VM or resource pool is guaranteed. This ensures that critical VMs always have access to a certain level of CPU resources.

Limits: Place an upper boundary on CPU resource consumption for a VM or resource pool. Even if excess CPU is available, the VM cannot use more than its limit.

Example: A high-priority VM running a database application might have 4,000 CPU shares, a reservation of 2 GHz, and a limit of 8 GHz. This ensures the VM receives at least 2 GHz of CPU, and during periods of contention, it is given priority over lower-share VMs.

Memory Allocation

Memory allocation works similarly to CPU allocation:

Shares: Control the relative importance of VMs during memory contention. VMs with more shares are prioritized when memory resources are scarce.

Reservations: Guarantee a certain amount of memory for a VM or resource pool. Reserved memory is always available, even during resource contention.

Limits: Define the maximum amount of memory a VM or resource pool can consume, regardless of available resources.

Example: A mission-critical application may have a memory reservation of 8 GB, ensuring that the application has adequate memory at all times. Meanwhile, less important VMs might have lower reservations or none at all, allowing them to share memory opportunistically.

Storage Allocation

Storage allocation in vSphere focuses on providing adequate disk space for VMs and ensuring that storage I/O is distributed fairly:

Storage Policies: Administrators can apply storage policies to ensure that VMs are provisioned on appropriate datastores based on performance, availability, or capacity needs.

Storage I/O Control (SIOC): This feature manages storage I/O shares to prioritize access to storage resources for critical VMs during periods of I/O contention.

Example: A VM running a transaction-heavy database application can be assigned a high share of storage I/O resources, ensuring it receives fast access to the storage system during peak usage periods.

Best Practices for Resource Management in Highly Virtualized Environments

To ensure efficient resource management in large-scale vSphere environments, follow these best practices:

Monitor Resource Utilization Regularly: Use tools like vRealize Operations Manager to monitor CPU, memory, and storage utilization across the environment. This helps detect resource bottlenecks and underutilization early.

Set Reservations for Critical Applications: For mission-critical applications, set CPU and memory reservations to guarantee that they always have access to the necessary resources, even during periods of contention.

Use Shares Wisely: Assign shares based on the relative importance of VMs or resource pools. During resource contention, shares will determine which VMs or pools get priority. Avoid setting shares too high for unimportant VMs.

Avoid Setting Limits Unnecessarily: Setting CPU or memory limits can artificially restrict the resources available to a VM, potentially leading to performance degradation. Use limits only when necessary to control resource usage.

Plan for Overcommitment: In environments where resource overcommitment (allocating more resources than physically available) is used, ensure that there is adequate capacity to handle spikes in resource demand without degrading performance.

Use Resource Pools for Organization: Organize VMs into resource pools based on business needs or application groups. Use nested pools for finer control and easier management.

Implement Storage I/O Control (SIOC): Enable SIOC to manage storage I/O contention. This ensures that high-priority VMs get faster access to storage resources when needed.

POTENTIAL EXAM QUESTIONS FOCUSED ON RESOURCE POOLS

In the VMware vSphere 8.x Professional exam, resource pools and resource allocation are likely to appear in various forms. Here are some example questions that could be on the exam:

What is the primary purpose of a resource pool in VMware vSphere?

> ➢ This question tests a candidate's understanding of the role that resource pools play in allocating and managing resources in a virtualized environment.

How does vSphere manage CPU contention between VMs in a resource pool?

> ➢ This question may focus on how vSphere uses shares, limits, and reservations to prioritize CPU resources during periods of contention.

Explain how to configure a resource pool and allocate memory and CPU resources in a vSphere environment.

> ➢ This practical question may ask the candidate to describe the step-by-step process of creating a resource pool and configuring resource settings.

What are the advantages of using resource pools in large-scale environments?

➢ This question examines a candidate's understanding of the organizational and performance benefits of resource pools, especially in environments with multiple applications and departments.

P.S.

By mastering resource pools and resource allocation, candidates can confidently handle related questions on the certification exam while effectively managing resources in production environments.

Practicing with hands-on labs and vSphere environments can provide critical insights into resource pool configuration, ensuring you are well-prepared for both the certification exam and real-world deployment.

vSphere Distributed Resource Scheduler (DRS)

VMware vSphere Distributed Resource Scheduler (DRS) is a key feature designed to optimize resource usage and improve the performance of virtualized environments. It automates the process of balancing virtual machine (VM) workloads across multiple ESXi hosts in a cluster by dynamically adjusting resource allocation based on current demand. By redistributing VMs in response to changes in resource usage, DRS helps to ensure that no single host becomes overburdened, improving overall system performance and efficiency.

<u>How DRS Works</u>

DRS continuously monitors resource utilization (such as CPU, memory, and network bandwidth) across the ESXi hosts in a cluster. It collects real-time data on resource consumption and workload patterns, allowing it to make informed decisions on the distribution of VMs. When imbalances are detected, DRS takes one of two actions:

➢ **VM Migration (vMotion):** DRS uses vMotion, VMware's live migration technology, to automatically move VMs from heavily loaded hosts to hosts with more available resources.

> **Initial Placement:** When new VMs are powered on, DRS chooses the best host for the VM based on current resource availability and the VM's requirements.

These actions are based on a set of predefined rules and policies that administrators can configure, allowing them to customize how DRS behaves according to the needs of their environment.

Key Components of DRS

Resource Distribution: DRS distributes resources dynamically, ensuring that workloads are spread across hosts to minimize contention and maximize performance. It calculates the resource demand of each VM and redistributes VMs accordingly, without requiring manual intervention.

Balancing Workloads: By constantly assessing the resource usage of hosts, DRS ensures that no host becomes a bottleneck. For instance, if one host's CPU or memory usage becomes too high, DRS can migrate VMs to less utilized hosts to achieve balance.

Load Prediction: In addition to real-time adjustments, DRS can predict future resource needs based on historical usage patterns. This allows DRS to make proactive adjustments to resource allocations, further improving performance.

DRS Automation Levels

DRS can operate in various automation levels, which define the degree to which DRS is allowed to automatically manage resource distribution. The automation levels are as follows:

Manual: In this mode, DRS makes recommendations for VM migrations, but it does not perform any actions automatically. The administrator must manually approve and initiate any suggested migrations.

Partially Automated: DRS automatically selects the best host for the initial placement of VMs when they are powered on. However, for subsequent load balancing decisions, DRS will only make recommendations, and the administrator must approve them.

Fully Automated: This is the highest level of automation, where DRS automatically handles both the initial placement of VMs and any subsequent load balancing migrations without requiring administrative approval. DRS makes decisions based on real-time data and predefined rules, ensuring that resource usage is optimized with minimal manual intervention.

P.S.

For large-scale environments with many VMs, Fully Automated mode is often the preferred option because it reduces administrative overhead and ensures that resources are continuously optimized. However, in sensitive environments where administrators want tighter control, Manual or Partially Automated modes might be more appropriate.

Configuring DRS Settings

DRS is enabled and configured at the cluster level within vSphere. Once DRS is enabled, administrators can adjust its settings to tailor how it operates based on their specific needs. Below are some of the key configuration options available when setting up DRS:

DRS Automation Level (Cluster-Wide):

Set the default level of automation for the entire cluster. This determines how much control DRS has over load balancing and VM placement. The three automation levels (Manual, Partially Automated, Fully Automated) provide different levels of control, as discussed earlier.

Migration Threshold:

DRS allows administrators to set a migration threshold, which determines how aggressively DRS should balance resources across the cluster. The migration threshold ranges from 1 (Conservative) to 5 (Aggressive):

> ➤ A Conservative setting (level 1) will only migrate VMs when there is a significant resource imbalance.
> ➤ An Aggressive setting (level 5) will result in more frequent migrations, even for relatively small imbalances. This may improve performance but could lead to increased vMotion overhead.

Resource Pools and Shares:

Resource pools can be used in conjunction with DRS to define how resources are allocated between different groups of VMs. By assigning shares, limits, and reservations to resource pools, administrators can prioritize certain VMs over others based on their importance.

For example, critical VMs running business applications might have more CPU shares, ensuring they receive more resources during times of contention, while less critical VMs may be allocated fewer shares.

Affinity and Anti-Affinity Rules:

DRS supports affinity and anti-affinity rules, which control where VMs are placed within the cluster:

Affinity rules ensure that certain VMs are always kept together on the same host.

Anti-affinity rules ensure that specific VMs are always placed on separate hosts. This is particularly useful for high-availability scenarios, where placing VMs on separate hosts ensures that the failure of one host does not affect multiple VMs.

Optimizing Resource Usage with DRS

In large environments, DRS plays a crucial role in optimizing resource usage and ensuring high availability. Below are examples of how DRS can be used to enhance performance and availability:

Balancing CPU and Memory Loads:

In environments where VMs are dynamically created or deleted, resource usage can fluctuate significantly. DRS ensures that workloads are distributed across the cluster to avoid overburdening any single host. This is particularly important when certain VMs require more CPU or memory during specific periods of the day.

Proactive Host Maintenance:

DRS can be used in conjunction with vSphere High Availability (HA) to minimize the impact of host failures. If a host requires maintenance, DRS can automatically evacuate all VMs from the host and redistribute them across other hosts in the cluster. This reduces downtime and simplifies maintenance tasks.

Ensuring High Availability:

By pairing DRS with affinity/anti-affinity rules, administrators can ensure that critical VMs are distributed across different hosts for redundancy. This setup is essential in high-availability environments, such as those running critical business applications, where downtime must be minimized.

EXAM TIPS FOR UNDERSTANDING DRS

The VMware vSphere 8.x Professional certification exam often includes questions on DRS, its configuration, and its role in optimizing resource usage. Here are some important concepts to keep in mind when preparing for the exam:

Automation Levels: Understand the differences between the Manual, Partially Automated, and Fully Automated modes. Be prepared to explain scenarios where each level would be appropriate.

Migration Threshold: Be familiar with how the migration threshold works and how adjusting it affects the frequency of vMotion migrations in the cluster.

Affinity Rules: Be ready to answer questions about affinity and anti-affinity rules, including how they are configured and when they should be used to ensure workload placement and availability.

DRS with Resource Pools: Recognize how resource pools can be used with DRS to ensure that specific groups of VMs receive the appropriate resources based on organizational priorities.

P.S.

Regular hands-on practice in a lab environment is crucial for mastering DRS configuration and management. Running test scenarios with different DRS settings will help you gain confidence for the certification exam and practical deployments.

Managing High Availability (HA) Clusters in VMware vSphere 8.x

VMware vSphere's High Availability (HA) feature is designed to reduce downtime and improve the availability of virtual machines (VMs) in a virtualized infrastructure. In a vSphere HA cluster, if an ESXi host fails, vSphere HA automatically restarts the VMs on other available hosts within the cluster, ensuring that business-critical applications remain accessible. HA provides protection against both host failures and guest operating system failures, allowing IT environments to maintain high uptime even in the face of hardware or software issues.

In vSphere 8.x, HA includes advanced features like Proactive HA and Admission Control policies, which enhance cluster resiliency and optimize resource utilization. This section covers the configuration and management of HA clusters, along with troubleshooting tips and potential exam scenarios related to HA.

How vSphere HA Works

VMware vSphere HA monitors the state of ESXi hosts in a cluster and automatically takes action when a failure occurs. Here's a breakdown of how HA works:

Host Failure Detection:

HA uses a mechanism called heartbeat monitoring to continuously check the availability of each ESXi host in the cluster. If a host stops sending heartbeats, vSphere HA assumes that the host has failed.

VM Restart on Another Host:

When a host failure is detected, HA automatically restarts the VMs that were running on the failed host on other available hosts in the cluster. This restart process minimizes downtime for the VMs, ensuring that critical services remain operational.

Application Monitoring:

vSphere HA also includes VM Monitoring, which tracks the health of applications running within VMs. If an application or guest operating system becomes unresponsive, HA can restart the affected VM on the same or another host within the cluster.

Configuring HA Clusters in vSphere 8.x

To configure an HA cluster in VMware vSphere 8.x, follow these steps:

Step 1: Enable HA on the Cluster

a. Log into the vSphere Client:
    ➤ Log into the vSphere Client and navigate to the Hosts and Clusters view.

b. Create or Select a Cluster:
    ➤ Either create a new cluster or select an existing one to enable HA.

c. Enable vSphere HA:
  ➢ Right-click the cluster and select Settings. Under the vSphere Availability section, check the box to Turn on vSphere HA.

d. Configure Cluster Settings:
  ➢ After enabling HA, configure the HA cluster settings. These settings include admission control, VM monitoring, and heartbeat datastore settings, which we'll explore in more detail below.

Step 2: Admission Control Policies

Admission Control ensures that the cluster reserves sufficient resources to restart VMs in the event of a host failure. Without proper admission control, the cluster could become overcommitted, leaving insufficient resources to restart all VMs after a failure.

There are three common admission control policies

a. Host Failures Cluster Tolerates:

This policy reserves enough resources to accommodate the loss of a specific number of hosts. For example, if the cluster is configured to tolerate one host failure, it ensures that sufficient CPU and memory resources are reserved to restart all VMs on the remaining hosts.

b. Percentage-Based Policy:

Instead of specifying the number of hosts, this policy reserves a percentage of cluster resources for failover purposes. For example, setting the policy to reserve 25% of cluster resources ensures that 25% of the CPU and memory are available for VM restarts.

c. Dedicated Failover Hosts:

In this configuration, one or more hosts are designated as failover hosts. These hosts remain idle during normal operations and are only used to run VMs when another host fails.

Step 3: VM Monitoring Settings

vSphere HA provides VM Monitoring, which checks the health of the guest operating system and applications running within VMs. If a VM stops responding to network pings or VMware Tools heartbeats, HA can take corrective action by restarting the VM. VM Monitoring settings include:

> **VM Monitoring Sensitivity:** This setting determines how aggressively HA monitors VMs for failures. A higher sensitivity results in more frequent monitoring.

> **Restart Priority:** Administrators can assign VMs a restart priority, ensuring that critical VMs are restarted first during failover situations. For example, database servers and application servers may have a higher priority than test *VMs*.

Step 4: Proactive HA

Proactive HA, introduced in vSphere 6.5 and enhanced in 8.x, goes a step beyond traditional HA by addressing hardware degradation before it leads to complete host failure. It integrates with hardware management tools (such as Dell EMC OpenManage or HPE Insight), which can notify vSphere of potential hardware issues such as failing power supplies or network cards.

When Proactive HA detects degraded hardware, it places the affected host into Quarantine Mode or Maintenance Mode:

> **Quarantine Mode:** The host continues running its existing VMs but avoids receiving new workloads. This ensures minimal disruption while preventing overloading healthy hosts.

> **Maintenance Mode:** The host is fully evacuated, with all running VMs migrated to other hosts in the cluster.

Proactive HA helps reduce the impact of hardware failures by ensuring that VMs are protected even before a complete failure occurs.

Troubleshooting Common HA Cluster Issues

While HA is highly reliable, issues can sometimes occur. Below are common problems that administrators may face when managing HA clusters and how to troubleshoot them:

Insufficient Resources to Restart VMs:

This issue typically arises when the cluster lacks sufficient resources (CPU, memory) to restart all the VMs after a host failure. To resolve this, ensure that admission control is correctly configured to reserve enough failover capacity. Reducing resource overcommitment (e.g., by lowering VM memory reservations) can also help.

HA Agent Failure:

Sometimes, the HA agent on an ESXi host may fail or become unresponsive. This can lead to VMs not being restarted after a host failure. Restart the HA agent using the Management Interface or SSH to resolve this issue. If necessary, reconfigure HA for the affected host.

Network Isolation:

vSphere HA relies on heartbeat signals between hosts to detect failures. If a host becomes isolated from the network (e.g., due to a switch failure), HA may incorrectly trigger VM failovers. To prevent this, configure Datastore Heartbeats, which allow HA to verify host status via shared storage when network heartbeats fail.

Failed VM Restarts:

If a VM fails to restart after a host failure, check the cluster logs to identify the cause. This could be due to insufficient resources, storage access issues, or VM-level restrictions (such as incorrect affinity rules). Ensuring proper configuration of VM restart priorities can also help.

EXAM TIPS FOR UNDERSTANDING HA CLUSTERS

The VMware vSphere 8.x Professional exam typically includes questions on configuring and managing HA clusters. Here are some key areas to focus on when preparing for the exam:

Admission Control Policies: Understand how admission control policies work and when to use each policy. Be familiar with the differences between the Host Failures Cluster Tolerates, Percentage-Based, and Dedicated Failover Host policies.

Proactive HA: Know how Proactive HA works and how it integrates with hardware monitoring tools. Be prepared to explain how Quarantine Mode and Maintenance Mode are used to protect VMs during hardware degradation.

Troubleshooting HA Issues: The exam may present scenarios where you need to troubleshoot HA-related issues, such as insufficient resources, agent failures, or network isolation. Be comfortable with diagnosing and resolving these issues.

VM Monitoring: Understand how VM Monitoring works and how to configure restart priorities to ensure that critical VMs are restarted first in the event of a failure.

P.S.

Hands-on experience with HA clusters is invaluable for mastering these concepts. Setting up a lab environment and practicing with various failure scenarios will help you better understand how HA behaves and how to troubleshoot potential issues.

MONITORING AND OPTIMIZING CPU/MEMORY RESOURCES IN VMWARE VSPHERE 8.X

In VMware vSphere 8.x, efficient management and optimization of CPU and memory resources are critical to maintaining optimal performance in virtualized environments. Given the dynamic nature of virtual machine (VM) workloads, CPU and memory usage can fluctuate significantly. Monitoring these resources and identifying bottlenecks are essential steps to ensuring smooth operations and avoiding performance degradation.

VMware provides a variety of tools for monitoring and optimizing resource usage. This section will explore the key tools available for performance monitoring, such as vSphere Performance Charts and ESXTOP, and best practices for managing CPU and memory resources effectively.

Tools for Monitoring CPU and Memory Resources

1. vSphere Performance Charts

vSphere Performance Charts provide an intuitive interface for monitoring CPU and memory usage at both the host and VM levels. These charts are accessible through the vSphere Client and allow administrators to quickly identify resource utilization patterns and spot potential bottlenecks.

Host Performance Monitoring:

At the host level, performance charts display metrics such as CPU usage (MHz) and memory usage (MB). Administrators can view real-time and historical data, helping them understand overall resource consumption trends across the entire ESXi host. Key performance metrics include:

- **CPU Usage (%):** The percentage of the CPU's total capacity in use by VMs.
- **Memory Usage (%):** The percentage of memory resources in use.
- **Co-Stop:** Co-stop measures how long a VM waits to schedule all its vCPUs simultaneously, which can indicate CPU contention.

VM-Level Performance Monitoring:

Performance charts at the VM level provide detailed insights into individual VM resource consumption. Administrators can track CPU and memory usage per VM, as well as identify metrics like memory ballooning (when the VMkernel reclaims memory) and swapping (when memory is swapped to disk), both of which may indicate memory contention.

Using vSphere Performance Charts to Identify Bottlenecks:

- A high CPU usage percentage (above 85-90%) at the host level may indicate a CPU bottleneck, meaning that the ESXi host's CPU resources are fully utilized and VMs may experience slow performance.
- Memory ballooning or swapping suggests that memory is overcommitted, forcing the ESXi host to reclaim or swap memory, which can degrade VM performance.

2. ESXTOP

ESXTOP is a powerful command-line utility for real-time monitoring of resource usage at a more granular level. It provides detailed information on CPU, memory, disk, and network performance. Administrators can use ESXTOP to monitor specific performance metrics that may not be immediately apparent in vSphere Performance Charts.

CPU Metrics in ESXTOP:

%RDY: This metric shows the percentage of time that a VM is ready to run but is waiting for CPU resources. High %RDY values indicate CPU contention.

%CSTP: Co-Stop time, which indicates the time VMs with multiple vCPUs are waiting to synchronize all their virtual CPUs.

Memory Metrics in ESXTOP:

MEMCTL (Ballooning): This column shows how much memory is being reclaimed from a VM via ballooning. A high value indicates memory pressure.

SWAP: This metric shows the amount of memory that is swapped to disk, which can significantly impact performance if swapping occurs frequently.

Using ESXTOP to Identify Bottlenecks:

- A high %RDY value (greater than 10%) suggests CPU contention, indicating that VMs are waiting for CPU resources to become available.
- High levels of ballooning or swapping indicate memory contention, where the host is under pressure to provide adequate memory resources.

Best Practices for Optimizing CPU and Memory Resources

1. Right-Sizing VMs

Right-sizing VMs involves configuring them with the correct amount of CPU and memory resources based on their actual usage patterns. Over-provisioning VMs with more vCPUs or memory than necessary can lead to resource contention and wasted resources, while under-provisioning can degrade performance.

a. CPU Right-Sizing:

Assigning too many vCPUs to a VM can result in CPU scheduling delays, especially if the host is overcommitted. Right-sizing involves reducing the number of vCPUs to match the actual demand. VMs should only be assigned the number of vCPUs they can use efficiently.

b. Memory Right-Sizing:

Similar to CPU, VMs should be allocated just enough memory to meet their needs. If a VM is using much less memory than allocated, it might lead to unnecessary memory overcommitment on the host. Right-sizing memory allocation reduces the likelihood of ballooning and swapping.

2. Use Resource Allocation Settings

VMware vSphere allows administrators to control how resources are allocated to VMs through shares, reservations, and limits.

a. Shares:

Shares define the relative importance of a VM compared to other VMs. In times of resource contention, VMs with higher shares receive a greater proportion of resources. For example, a mission-critical database server might be assigned more CPU shares than a test VM to ensure it always receives priority during high demand.

b. Reservations:

Reservations guarantee that a specific amount of CPU or memory is set aside for a VM, regardless of contention on the host. For example, setting a CPU reservation of 2 GHz ensures that the VM always has access to at least 2 GHz of CPU power.

c. Limits:

Limits cap the maximum amount of CPU or memory that a VM can consume. Administrators should use limits sparingly, as they can restrict VMs from utilizing additional resources when available, potentially degrading performance unnecessarily.

3. Avoid Overcommitment

Overcommitting CPU and memory resources—allocating more resources than are physically available—can lead to contention and poor performance, especially under heavy workloads. To avoid overcommitment:

a. Monitor CPU and Memory Utilization:

Regularly monitor CPU and memory usage on the host and VMs. If the CPU Ready or memory swapping metrics are high, reduce overcommitment by adjusting VM configurations or adding more physical resources to the host.

b. Use DRS for Load Balancing:

VMware's Distributed Resource Scheduler (DRS) can help balance workloads across hosts in a cluster, reducing the likelihood of resource contention on a single host. DRS can automatically migrate VMs between hosts to ensure optimal resource distribution based on current CPU and memory usage.

4. Use CPU and Memory Hot Add

In vSphere 8.x, administrators can enable CPU and Memory Hot Add, which allows them to add CPU and memory to a VM without shutting it down. This feature is particularly useful in dynamic environments where workloads may spike unexpectedly, allowing for rapid resource scaling without impacting uptime.

5. Monitor and Optimize vCPU/Memory Ratios

VMware recommends monitoring the vCPU-to-pCPU ratio (virtual CPUs to physical CPUs) in virtualized environments. A high vCPU-to-pCPU ratio can lead to CPU contention, where VMs must wait longer for physical CPU time. A general guideline is to maintain a ratio of 4:1 or 5:1 (vCPUs to pCPUs), though this can vary based on workload type.

P.S.

For memory, ensuring that the memory-to-VM density is balanced is important to prevent overcommitting memory, which can lead to swapping or ballooning. Regularly reviewing memory metrics will help ensure that resources are appropriately allocated and used efficiently.

Practical Tips for Fine-Tuning CPU and Memory Resources

Check CPU Ready Time:

Keep an eye on CPU Ready Time in both vSphere Performance Charts and ESXTOP. High ready times (above 10%) are a strong indicator of CPU contention, and reducing the number of vCPUs assigned to VMs can alleviate the issue.

Leverage Transparent Page Sharing (TPS):

Transparent Page Sharing (TPS) allows ESXi to deduplicate identical memory pages across multiple VMs, freeing up memory resources. Ensure TPS is enabled to optimize memory usage, especially in environments with many similar VMs.

Optimize NUMA Settings:

In systems with NUMA (Non-Uniform Memory Access) architectures, ensure that VMs are aligned with the NUMA node boundaries for optimal performance. Misaligned VMs may experience memory access latencies, degrading overall performance.

Monitor Ballooning and Swapping:

Ballooning and swapping are indicators of memory contention. While ballooning is less harmful than swapping, it still indicates that memory is overcommitted. Minimize both by right-sizing memory allocation and avoiding overcommitment.

LIKELY EXAM-RELATED QUESTIONS

For the VMware vSphere 8.x Professional certification exam, you can expect questions related to:

- Identifying CPU and memory bottlenecks using vSphere Performance Charts or ESXTOP.
- Understanding and configuring resource allocation settings such as shares, reservations, and limits.
- Addressing CPU contention by monitoring metrics like CPU Ready Time and Co-Stop.
- Recognizing the impact of memory ballooning and swapping on VM performance.
- Examining the role of vCPU-to-pCPU ratios and best practices for maintaining efficient resource allocation in highly virtualized environments.

P.S.

Gaining hands-on experience with monitoring tools like **ESOP and keeping overall resource allocation optimized for your virtual environment.

Storage and Network I/O Control in VMware vSphere 8.x

In modern virtualized environments, managing resource contention for both storage and network traffic is crucial to maintaining performance and efficiency. VMware vSphere 8.x introduces powerful features like Storage I/O Control (SIOC) and Network I/O Control (NIOC), which enable administrators to manage and prioritize resource allocation across multiple virtual machines (VMs) and hosts, ensuring fair distribution of resources even under heavy load. By configuring these controls, you can optimize performance in environments where competing workloads demand a higher degree of resource management.

Storage I/O Control (SIOC)

Storage I/O Control (SIOC) is a feature in vSphere that provides granular control over storage performance by dynamically allocating I/O resources among VMs based on their configured priorities and actual usage. SIOC ensures that VMs with higher priority or critical workloads receive the necessary storage resources during periods of contention, preventing resource-hungry VMs from monopolizing storage bandwidth at the expense of others.

How SIOC Works

SIOC monitors storage latency on datastores and triggers resource controls when latency exceeds a predefined threshold (known as the congestion threshold). When congestion occurs, SIOC dynamically adjusts the I/O allocation based on the shares assigned to each VM, similar to how CPU and memory shares work. VMs with higher shares receive more access to storage resources, while lower-priority VMs are limited to prevent them from degrading overall storage performance.

Configuring SIOC

To configure SIOC in vSphere 8.x, follow these steps:

Enable SIOC on a Datastore:

- In the vSphere Client, navigate to the Datastores view.
- Right-click the datastore on which you want to enable SIOC and select Settings.
- In the I/O Control tab, check the box to enable Storage I/O Control for the datastore.

Set the Congestion Threshold:

- vSphere sets a default congestion threshold (in milliseconds) that represents the latency limit for the datastore. If the latency exceeds this threshold, SIOC will begin prioritizing I/O requests.
- You can customize the threshold based on your storage environment. For example, SSDs can tolerate lower latency than traditional HDDs, so adjust the threshold accordingly.

Assign I/O Shares to VMs:

- For each VM, navigate to the VM Edit Settings page and configure the shares under the Hard Disk section.
- By default, VMs are assigned equal shares, but for mission-critical VMs, you may want to assign high shares, ensuring that they receive more I/O bandwidth during contention.

Example of SIOC in Action

Consider an environment where several VMs are sharing a high-performance SSD datastore. During peak usage, the datastore experiences high latency due to an I/O-intensive VM running a backup process. With SIOC enabled, the system detects the increase in latency and dynamically throttles the I/O of the backup VM, ensuring that other VMs running critical applications (such as databases) continue to receive the necessary storage resources.

Network I/O Control (NIOC)

Network I/O Control (NIOC) is a similar feature to SIOC, but it focuses on managing network bandwidth instead of storage resources. NIOC allows administrators to allocate and prioritize network traffic across various traffic types, such as vMotion, VM traffic, management traffic, and iSCSI/NFS storage traffic. NIOC helps ensure that critical network operations receive sufficient bandwidth during times of congestion, preventing lower-priority traffic from overwhelming the network.

How NIOC Works

NIOC classifies network traffic into multiple categories (or traffic types), such as vMotion, VM network, and Fault Tolerance (FT) traffic. Administrators can assign each traffic type a specific bandwidth share or limit, ensuring that higher-priority traffic is prioritized during times of network contention. NIOC operates at the vSphere Distributed Switch (vDS) level, providing centralized control over network resource allocation.

Configuring NIOC

To configure NIOC, follow these steps:

Enable NIOC on a Distributed Switch:

- In the vSphere Client, navigate to the Networking view and select the vSphere Distributed Switch (vDS) where you want to enable NIOC.
- Right-click the switch and choose Edit Settings.
- In the Resource Allocation tab, enable Network I/O Control.

Configure Network Resource Pools:

- By default, NIOC classifies network traffic into categories, such as Management, vMotion, VM Network, iSCSI, and NFS. You can adjust the bandwidth share for each type based on its importance in your environment.
- Assign shares and limits to each network resource pool. Shares determine the priority of each traffic type during contention, while limits cap the maximum bandwidth that a traffic type can consume.

Monitor NIOC Performance:

Use the vSphere Performance Charts or third-party monitoring tools to observe network traffic usage and ensure that critical traffic is receiving sufficient bandwidth.

Example of NIOC in Action

In a scenario where a vSphere environment is handling multiple network traffic types, such as vMotion during VM migrations, management traffic for administrative tasks, and VM traffic for end-user applications, NIOC ensures that VM traffic continues to operate smoothly even when vMotion generates a large amount of network traffic. By prioritizing VM traffic over vMotion traffic, NIOC prevents disruptions to production workloads while still allowing VM migrations to occur without manual intervention.

Best Practices for Configuring SIOC and NIOC

1. Monitor Resource Utilization Regularly

Both SIOC and NIOC rely on real-time monitoring of I/O and network traffic. Regularly review vSphere Performance Charts and other monitoring tools to identify potential bottlenecks before they impact performance. Use these insights to fine-tune shares and limits based on workload needs.

2. Avoid Overcommitting Resources

While vSphere enables resource overcommitment to a certain extent, overcommitting network and storage resources can lead to severe performance degradation. Use shares and limits conservatively to prevent low-priority workloads from consuming excessive I/O or bandwidth, leaving insufficient resources for critical operations.

3. Balance Shares Appropriately

Ensure that shares for network and storage resources are allocated based on the importance of each VM or traffic type. For example, database traffic should receive higher shares than test VMs, and management traffic should be prioritized over bulk backup traffic.

4. Use Appropriate Congestion Thresholds

For SIOC, set appropriate congestion thresholds based on your storage environment. SSDs and all-flash arrays can tolerate lower latencies than HDD-based arrays, so adjust the threshold accordingly to avoid unnecessary throttling of I/O.

5. Test Changes in a Controlled Environment

Before implementing changes to SIOC or NIOC settings in a production environment, test the configurations in a controlled or test environment. This allows you to observe the effects of different share and limit configurations without disrupting production workloads.

EXAM TIPS FOR MANAGING NETWORK AND STORAGE RESOURCES

The VMware vSphere 8.x Professional certification exam may include questions that test your understanding of SIOC and NIOC, as well as their configuration and impact on resource management. Here are some key areas to focus on for the exam:

- **Understanding the Purpose of SIOC and NIOC:** Be prepared to explain how SIOC and NIOC help manage resource contention for storage and network traffic in a vSphere environment.

- **Configuring Shares, Limits, and Reservations:** Understand how to configure shares and limits for both network and storage traffic, and how these settings impact performance under resource contention.

- **Identifying and Resolving Bottlenecks:** Be familiar with the metrics used to identify I/O and network bottlenecks, such as storage latency (for SIOC) and network throughput (for NIOC).

- **Best Practices for Optimization:** Know the best practices for configuring SIOC and NIOC to ensure optimal performance in environments with competing workloads.

P.S.

Practical experience in configuring and optimizing SIOC and NIOC is crucial for mastering these concepts. Use Vmware labs or a sandbox environment to test different configurations and observe how they impact performance in real-world scenarios.

Troubleshooting Performance Issues in Vmware vSphere 8.x

Performance issues in Vmware vSphere environments can impact the efficiency of workloads and degrade the overall experience for users. Common problems arise in areas such as CPU, memory, storage, and networking. Effective troubleshooting requires a combination of the right tools and best practices to quickly identify and resolve these issues.

In this section, we'll explore the most common performance problems encountered in vSphere environments, the tools used for troubleshooting (like vSphere Client, ESXTOP, and vRealize Operations), and best practices for resolving these issues. This knowledge is also essential for preparing for the vSphere 8.x Professional certification exam, which may include questions about identifying and resolving performance problems.

Common Performance Problems

4. CPU-Related Performance Issues

Symptoms: High CPU ready time (the time a virtual machine is ready to run but waiting for CPU resources), CPU contention, or high overall CPU usage on ESXi hosts.

Common Causes:

- **Over-provisioning of vCPUs:** Assigning too many virtual CPUs to VMs relative to the number of available physical CPUs (pCPUs) can lead to contention and increased CPU ready times.
- **High CPU demand from specific VMs:** A single VM may be consuming more CPU resources than expected, impacting the performance of other VMs on the host.

Troubleshooting Steps:

vSphere Client:

- Navigate to the Host and Clusters view in the vSphere Client.
- Check the CPU Usage (%) and CPU Ready (%) metrics for both the host and VMs. High CPU ready times (greater than 10%) indicate contention.

ESXTOP:

Use ESXTOP to monitor CPU performance. Key metrics include:

- **%RDY:** Shows how long VMs are waiting for CPU resources. High values indicate CPU contention.
- **%CSTP:** The co-stop metric indicates issues with vCPU scheduling on multi-vCPU VMs.

If %RDY exceeds 10%, reduce the number of vCPUs assigned to the VMs, right-size workloads, or migrate VMs to other hosts to balance the load.

2. Memory-Related Performance Issues

Symptoms: Memory swapping (where memory is paged out to disk), memory ballooning (where the hypervisor reclaims memory from VMs), or high memory usage.

Common Causes:

- **Overcommitting memory resources on the host:** Assigning more virtual memory to VMs than is physically available on the ESXi host can lead to ballooning and swapping, which degrades performance.
- Large memory-intensive workloads without sufficient memory reservations.

Troubleshooting Steps:

vSphere Performance Charts:

- Use vSphere Performance Charts to monitor memory usage at both the host and VM levels.
- Look for Ballooning and Swapping metrics. If swapping is present, it indicates that the host is overcommitted on memory and is using disk storage to handle memory operations, which significantly impacts performance.

ESXTOP:

In ESXTOP, monitor the following memory metrics:

- **MEMCTL (Ballooning):** Shows the amount of memory being reclaimed via ballooning.
- **SWAP:** Shows the amount of memory being swapped to disk.

To resolve memory issues, either reduce the memory overcommitment, increase physical memory on the host, or adjust memory reservations for critical VMs.

5. Storage-Related Performance Issues

Symptoms: High storage latency, slow disk I/O performance, or datastore access issues.

Common Causes:

- **Storage I/O contention:** Multiple VMs accessing the same datastore may create bottlenecks, especially during intensive I/O operations.
- Poor configuration of Storage I/O Control (SIOC).
- Improperly configured storage arrays or datastores.

Troubleshooting Steps:

vSphere Performance Charts:

Monitor Disk Usage and Datastore Latency metrics. High latency values (typically above 20-30ms) indicate a storage bottleneck.

ESXTOP:

Use ESXTOP to monitor disk I/O performance. Key metrics include:

- **GAVG/cmd (Guest Average Latency):** High values indicate performance issues from the VM perspective.
- **KAVG/cmd (Kernel Average Latency):** High values suggest delays in the ESXi host kernel.
- **DAVG/cmd (Device Average Latency):** High values point to delays at the storage device level.

To resolve storage issues, use SIOC to prioritize critical workloads, optimize datastore configurations, and check the underlying storage array for issues.

6. Network-Related Performance Issues

Symptoms: High network latency, packet loss, or slow network performance for VMs.

Common Causes:

- **Network bandwidth contention:** Multiple VMs or processes (e.g., vMotion traffic) competing for bandwidth on the same network adapters can cause congestion.
- Improper Network I/O Control (NIOC) configuration.

Troubleshooting Steps:

vSphere Client:

- Use the vSphere Performance Charts to monitor network throughput, packet loss, and dropped packets on both the VM and host levels.
- High packet drop rates indicate contention or configuration issues.

ESXTOP:

- In ESXTOP, look at the NETWORK tab to check network traffic metrics such as throughput (Mbps) and packet loss.
- If network contention is present, configure NIOC to prioritize critical traffic types, such as VM or management traffic, over less critical traffic (e.g., backup or replication traffic).

<u>vSphere Distributed Switch (vDS):</u>

If using a vSphere Distributed Switch (vDS), ensure that Network I/O Control (NIOC) is enabled and configured correctly to prioritize traffic types like vMotion, VM network, and storage traffic.

Best Practices for Troubleshooting Performance Issues

7. Use vRealize Operations for Proactive Monitoring

vRealize Operations is a powerful tool for monitoring and optimizing performance across the vSphere environment. It provides advanced analytics, alerts, and capacity planning tools to help identify issues before they impact workloads. By setting up thresholds and alerts, administrators can proactively address potential performance bottlenecks.

2. Right-Size VMs

One of the most common causes of performance issues is improperly sized VMs. Over-provisioning or under-provisioning vCPUs or memory can lead to contention, ballooning, swapping, and CPU ready times. Regularly assess VM workloads and right-size VMs to align resource allocation with actual demand.

8. Use Distributed Resource Scheduler (DRS)

DRS automatically balances workloads across multiple hosts, helping prevent resource contention. When performance issues arise due to overloading on a single host, DRS can migrate VMs to other hosts with available resources. Ensure that DRS is properly configured with fully automated mode and the appropriate aggressiveness setting.

9. Avoid Overcommitment of Resources

While vSphere allows for resource overcommitment, excessive overcommitment can degrade performance. Regularly monitor CPU and memory usage to ensure that overcommitment does not lead to significant swapping, ballooning, or high CPU ready times. Proper use of reservations, limits, and shares can help mitigate the effects of overcommitment.

EXAM-RELEVANT QUESTIONS

When preparing for the Vmware vSphere 8.x Professional certification exam, understanding performance troubleshooting is crucial. Expect questions on the following topics:

- How to interpret CPU ready times, ballooning, and memory swapping metrics in vSphere Performance Charts and ESXTOP.

- Identifying the causes of network and storage latency and how to resolve them using NIOC and SIOC.

- Configuring DRS to balance workloads effectively and prevent CPU and memory contention.

- Understanding how to use vRealize Operations for proactive monitoring and alerting on performance issues.

P.S.

Hands-on experience with troubleshooting tools like ESXTOP and vRealize Operations is critical to mastering performance optimization. Practice identifying and resolving common performance problems in a lab environment to gain confidence for both real-world situations and the certification exam.

BEST PRACTICES FOR VSPHERE SECURITY IN VMWARE VSPHERE 8.X

Security is one of the most critical aspects of managing any IT infrastructure, and Vmware vSphere 8.x provides robust features and configurations to protect virtualized environments from threats. However, simply deploying vSphere is not enough to ensure security; administrators must follow best practices to secure ESXi hosts, vCenter Server, and virtual machines (VMs). In this section, we'll cover key security strategies, including implementing strong password policies, configuring firewalls, and hardening vSphere environments to minimize security risks. We will also explore how to prepare for exam-related questions about securing Vmware infrastructures.

10. Securing ESXi Hosts

ESXi hosts form the foundation of the virtualized infrastructure, and ensuring their security is paramount to protecting the entire environment.

a. Enable Secure Boot

Secure Boot is a feature that ensures only trusted and signed software components are loaded when the ESXi host starts up. By enabling Secure Boot, administrators prevent unauthorized code or tampered components from being executed.

To enable Secure Boot:

- Ensure the ESXi host's BIOS/UEFI supports Secure Boot and that it is enabled.
- Enable Secure Boot in the ESXi Host Profile via vSphere Client or during the host's installation.

b. Lockdown Mode

Lockdown Mode limits access to the ESXi host, ensuring that it can only be managed through vCenter Server. This reduces the risk of unauthorized access to the host and enforces a more centralized management model.

There are two levels of Lockdown Mode:

- ➤ **Normal Lockdown:** Prevents access to the ESXi host directly but still allows users with the DCUI (Direct Console User Interface) privilege to log in.

> **Strict Lockdown:** Prevents all direct access to the host, including DCUI access.

To enable Lockdown Mode:

- Go to the vSphere Client.
- Navigate to Host > Configure > Security Profile.
- Enable Lockdown Mode and select the appropriate level (Normal or Strict).

c. Limit Management Access

By default, SSH and the ESXi Shell are disabled. These services should remain disabled unless actively needed for troubleshooting, as leaving them open increases the attack surface of the ESXi host.

To manage SSH and ESXi Shell access:

- Go to vSphere Client > Host > Configure > Security Profile.
- Under Services, disable SSH and ESXi Shell.

d. Firewall Configuration

The ESXi firewall controls incoming and outgoing traffic to services running on the ESXi host. Vmware recommends only enabling the specific services required for your environment and blocking all unnecessary ports to minimize vulnerabilities.

To configure the ESXi firewall:

- Go to vSphere Client > Host > Configure > Security Profile.
- Under Firewall, review and configure which services are allowed to access the host.

e. Use Strong Password Policies

Ensuring strong password policies for the root account and other users with host access is critical to preventing unauthorized access. Vmware recommends:

- Enforcing complex passwords (e.g., minimum length, special characters).
- Regularly rotating passwords.
- Disabling or locking unused accounts.

In vCenter Server, you can configure password complexity rules for ESXi hosts by using Host Profiles or via the vSphere Client.

2. Securing vCenter Server

vCenter Server is the central management platform for vSphere environments, and securing it is crucial for maintaining overall infrastructure security.

a. vCenter Server Appliance (VCSA) Security

vCenter Server Appliance (VCSA) is the preferred deployment method for vCenter, and it includes several built-in security features:

- **Built-in Firewall:** VCSA has a built-in firewall that can be configured to restrict access to vCenter services.
- **Single Sign-On (SSO):** Configuring SSO with strong passwords and integrating it with Active Directory (AD) or LDAP enhances identity management and security.

b. Enforce Role-Based Access Control (RBAC)

Vmware recommends using Role-Based Access Control (RBAC) to limit access to vCenter resources. Instead of assigning administrative privileges to every user, administrators should define custom roles and assign the minimum necessary permissions. For example:

- Administrators may have full access to manage clusters and hosts.
- VM Operators may only have access to manage VMs without modifying host settings.
- By minimizing user privileges based on roles, you reduce the risk of accidental or malicious changes to the environment.

c. Enable vCenter Server Alarms

vCenter includes built-in alarms to monitor security events, such as login failures, privilege escalations, or changes to configurations. Configuring these alarms to alert administrators in real-time helps detect potential security breaches early.

To configure alarms:

- Go to vCenter Server in the vSphere Client.
- Navigate to Alarms and create new alarm rules to monitor security events such as unauthorized access attempts or configuration changes.

11. Securing Virtual Machines (VMs)

VMs are the core of the virtualized environment, and securing them ensures that workloads running on the infrastructure are protected.

a. Use VM Encryption

In vSphere 8.x, administrators can encrypt virtual machines using vSphere VM Encryption. VM encryption protects sensitive data by ensuring that the VM's data (virtual disks, configurations, etc.) are encrypted at rest. Encryption also secures VMs from being accessed in unauthorized ways, even if the data is extracted outside of the vSphere environment.

To enable VM encryption:

- Set up a Key Management Server (KMS) to manage encryption keys.
- Use vSphere Client to encrypt VM disks and configurations.

b. Enable Secure Boot for VMs

Secure Boot for VMs ensures that only signed and trusted components (e.g., bootloaders and operating systems) are loaded within the virtual machine. Enabling this feature prevents tampered or unauthorized code from being executed.

To enable Secure Boot for VMs:

- Go to the VM Edit Settings page.
- Under the Boot Options tab, enable Secure Boot.

c. Limit VM Console Access

VM console access provides full control over the virtual machine, including the ability to restart, power off, or modify settings. Limiting console access to only authorized users ensures that only those with the necessary permissions can interact with critical VMs.

To limit VM console access:

- Use RBAC to define who can access VM consoles.
- Disable console access for non-administrative roles.

12. Hardening vSphere Environments

Hardening is the process of configuring systems to reduce their attack surface and eliminate potential vulnerabilities.

a. Use Vmware Security Hardening Guide

Vmware publishes a comprehensive vSphere Security Hardening Guide, which provides recommendations for securing different components of the vSphere environment, including ESXi, vCenter, and VMs. Following this guide helps administrators adhere to industry best practices and ensure compliance with security standards such as CIS or ISO.

b. Enable vSphere Audit Logging

Audit logging is essential for tracking activities within the vSphere environment. Enabling detailed logging ensures that all security-related events (e.g., configuration changes, user logins, etc.) are captured, which aids in monitoring and forensic investigations in the event of a security breach.

To enable and configure audit logging:

- Go to vCenter Server Settings in the vSphere Client.
- Navigate to Advanced Settings and configure detailed logging for security-related activities.

c. Network Segmentation and Isolation

Network segmentation reduces the attack surface by isolating critical network traffic, such as management, vMotion, storage, and VM traffic, into separate VLANs. By isolating sensitive network segments, administrators prevent attackers from moving laterally within the network.

Best Practices:

- Create separate VLANs for management, storage, and production workloads.
- Use firewalls and ACLs (Access Control Lists) to restrict access between segments.

EXAM PREPARATION TIPS

When preparing for the Vmware vSphere 8.x Professional certification exam, security is a key topic. Here are some tips to help you prepare:

- ➤ **Understand ESXi Host Security:** Be familiar with configuring Secure Boot, Lockdown Mode, and managing SSH/ESXi Shell access.

- ➤ **Know vCenter Server Security Best Practices:** Be able to explain how to configure RBAC, password policies, and alarms to detect unauthorized activity.

- ➤ **VM Encryption and Secure Boot:** Understand how to enable and manage VM encryption and Secure Boot to protect VM workloads.

- ➤ **Follow Vmware Hardening Guidelines:** Familiarize yourself with the vSphere Security Hardening Guide and be ready to apply best practices for securing virtualized environments.

P.S.

Hands-on experience is critical for mastering vSphere security. Setting up a lab environment where you can apply these security configurations will greatly enhance your understanding and preparation for the exam.

Configuring Vmware Trust Authority in vSphere 8.x

In Vmware vSphere 8.x, Vmware Trust Authority (vTA) plays a pivotal role in enhancing security by establishing a trusted infrastructure using hardware-based security modules like Trusted Platform Modules (TPM). Vmware Trust Authority helps ensure that only verified and trusted components can access and manage sensitive environments, making it a critical feature for organizations aiming to safeguard their virtual infrastructures. This section will explore the role of Vmware Trust Authority, how to configure it, the benefits it offers, and exam scenarios that might involve using Trust Authority to secure virtual environments.

What is Vmware Trust Authority?

VMware Trust Authority is a security framework that enhances the integrity of a vSphere environment by leveraging hardware-based security modules such as TPM 2.0 and Hardware Root of Trust. Trust Authority allows administrators to create a secure, trusted infrastructure by ensuring that only validated hosts and components are allowed to participate in the vSphere environment. Trust Authority is especially useful for high-security environments such as government, healthcare, or financial organizations, where regulatory compliance and security are paramount.

The core idea behind Trust Authority is to offload the task of attesting and verifying trusted infrastructure components, ensuring that only trusted ESXi hosts can manage workloads. This feature establishes a chain of trust from the hardware level up to the hypervisor, enhancing security by leveraging hardware-based attestation mechanisms.

Role of TPM (Trusted Platform Module)

The Trusted Platform Module (TPM) is a hardware device that provides secure storage for cryptographic keys and ensures the integrity of the boot process. TPM 2.0 is a critical component in VMware Trust Authority because it stores measurements taken during the boot process to verify that the host's hardware and software are trustworthy.

When an ESXi host with TPM 2.0 boots up, it records measurements (such as firmware, BIOS, and ESXi configurations) into the TPM chip. These measurements are then used by Trust Authority to validate that the host has not been tampered with and is running a secure, unmodified configuration. If the measurements don't match trusted values, the host is considered untrusted and cannot be allowed to participate in the infrastructure.

Configuring VMware Trust Authority

Configuring VMware Trust Authority in vSphere 8.x involves several steps, including setting up a Trust Authority cluster, configuring the ESXi hosts with TPM 2.0, and enabling attestation.

Step 1: Set Up a Trust Authority Cluster

The first step is to set up a separate Trust Authority Cluster (TA Cluster) in the vSphere environment. This cluster is responsible for managing the attestation and cryptographic operations necessary for ensuring trust in the infrastructure.

Deploy the Trust Authority Cluster:

- Create a new cluster in vCenter Server dedicated to Trust Authority.
- This cluster must consist of hosts that will be responsible for handling the Key Management Server (KMS) and attestation services.

Enable vSphere Native Key Provider:

- Trust Authority requires a Key Management Service (KMS) to manage encryption keys used for VM encryption and host attestation. vSphere 8.x offers a built-in Native Key Provider, which can be enabled for this purpose.

Configure TPM Support:

- Ensure that the hosts in the Trust Authority Cluster are equipped with TPM 2.0 hardware and that TPM support is enabled in the BIOS/UEFI settings.

Step 2: Configure Attestation

Once the Trust Authority Cluster is set up, the next step is to configure attestation, which is the process of verifying that ESXi hosts are running trusted and secure configurations.

Enable Host Attestation:

- For each host that you want to secure, enable Host Attestation in vCenter Server.
- Attestation involves checking the boot measurements stored in the TPM to ensure that the host has not been compromised.

Validate Host Measurements:

- During the attestation process, the host's TPM measurements are compared against trusted baseline measurements stored in the Trust Authority Cluster.
- If the measurements match, the host is considered trusted and allowed to run workloads. If they don't match, the host is flagged as untrusted and is prevented from participating in the cluster.

Step 3: Enforce Trust Authority Policies

Once Trust Authority is configured and attestation is in place, administrators can enforce security policies to ensure that only trusted hosts can manage critical workloads. This can include:

- **Restricting VMs to run only on trusted hosts:** Policies can be set to ensure that VMs are only deployed on hosts that have passed attestation, ensuring the integrity of the infrastructure.
- **Encrypting VMs:** Leverage the Native Key Provider or an external KMS to encrypt VMs, ensuring that only trusted hosts can access sensitive data.

Benefits of VMware Trust Authority

VMware Trust Authority offers several significant benefits to organizations seeking to secure their virtual infrastructure:

Hardware-Based Security: By leveraging TPM 2.0 and hardware-based attestation, Trust Authority ensures a higher level of security than software-only solutions. The trust is rooted in the hardware, providing more robust protection against tampering.

Chain of Trust: Trust Authority extends the chain of trust from the hardware layer to the hypervisor, ensuring that every layer in the infrastructure is secure. This is particularly important for high-security environments where the integrity of the platform is critical.

Simplified Compliance: By ensuring that only trusted hosts can participate in the infrastructure, Trust Authority helps organizations meet regulatory requirements for data security and compliance, such as GDPR, HIPAA, and PCI DSS.

Secure VM Encryption: Trust Authority integrates seamlessly with vSphere's encryption features, allowing administrators to encrypt VMs and guarantee that only trusted hosts can access them. This is essential for protecting sensitive workloads from unauthorized access.

EXAM-RELATED SCENARIOS INVOLVING VMWARE TRUST AUTHORITY

In the VMware vSphere 8.x Professional certification exam, you may encounter scenarios that test your understanding of VMware Trust Authority. Here are a few example questions that could appear:

How does VMware Trust Authority use TPM to ensure the security of ESXi hosts?

➤ This question might test your knowledge of how TPM stores boot measurements and how these measurements are validated through Trust Authority to ensure the integrity of the host.

What steps are required to configure a Trust Authority Cluster in a vSphere environment?

➤ This could involve questions about deploying a Trust Authority Cluster, enabling attestation, and enforcing trust policies for VMs and hosts.

How can Trust Authority help meet regulatory compliance requirements in a virtualized environment?

➤ This scenario might ask you to explain how hardware-based attestation and encryption contribute to securing sensitive workloads and ensuring compliance with industry standards.

P.S.

Hands-on practice is essential for mastering Trust Authority. Setting up a test environment where you can configure Trust Authority, enable TPM, and validate attestation policies will significantly enhance your understanding and help you prepare for exam questions on this topic.

vSphere Certificate Management in VMware vSphere 8.x

In VMware vSphere 8.x, SSL certificates play a critical role in securing communications between various components of the vSphere infrastructure, such as vCenter Server, ESXi hosts, and vSphere Clients. Proper certificate management is essential to ensure that all communication remains encrypted and secure. Managing certificates, whether self-signed or issued by a trusted Certificate Authority (CA), involves handling tasks like configuration, renewal, and troubleshooting. This section covers the fundamentals of vSphere certificate management, focusing on best practices for securing vSphere environments and how to manage certificates efficiently in a scalable infrastructure.

SSL Certificates in vSphere

SSL/TLS certificates in vSphere are used to secure and authenticate communication between different components. These certificates ensure that all data transmitted across the network is encrypted, preventing unauthorized access or interception of sensitive information. vSphere 8.x supports both self-signed certificates (automatically generated by vCenter Server) and certificates issued by a trusted Certificate Authority (CA).

Components Secured by SSL Certificates

a. vCenter Server:

vCenter Server uses certificates to secure communications between itself and vSphere Clients, ESXi hosts, and other integrated services.

b. ESXi Hosts:

Each ESXi host is assigned an SSL certificate that secures management traffic between the host, vCenter Server, and other administrative clients.

c. vSphere Web Client:

The vSphere Web Client uses certificates to establish secure HTTPS connections between administrators and vSphere infrastructure.

d. vSphere Replication, vMotion, and vSAN:

SSL certificates are used to secure communications in features like vSphere Replication, vMotion, and vSAN, where sensitive data is transmitted between hosts and clusters.

Configuring SSL Certificates in vSphere

1. vCenter Server Certificate Management

vCenter Server in vSphere 8.x includes a built-in VMware Certificate Authority (VMCA), which can manage certificates for vCenter components. Administrators can choose between using certificates generated by the VMCA or replacing them with custom certificates from an external CA.

a. VMCA-Signed Certificates:

By default, vCenter Server uses VMCA-signed certificates to secure communication between components. This method is suitable for most environments where internal trust is sufficient.

b. Custom CA-Signed Certificates:

For environments requiring certificates signed by a trusted external CA, administrators can replace the default VMCA-signed certificates with custom certificates. This is typically required in organizations that adhere to strict security policies or regulatory compliance standards (such as PCI DSS or HIPAA).

Steps to Replace Certificates with CA-Signed Certificates:

- **Generate a Certificate Signing Request (CSR):**

Use the vSphere Client or vCenter Server Certificate Manager to generate a CSR for the vCenter Server and its services.

- **Submit CSR to a CA:**

Submit the generated CSR to a trusted CA and obtain the signed certificates.

- **Replace Certificates in vCenter:**

Use the vCenter Server Certificate Manager to replace the existing certificates with the new CA-signed certificates. Ensure that all services (like vSphere Web Client and SSO) are restarted to apply the changes.

2. ESXi Host Certificate Management

Each ESXi host in the vSphere environment also requires an SSL certificate. Like vCenter Server, administrators can choose between using the VMCA or custom CA-signed certificates for ESXi hosts.

a. VMCA-Signed Certificates:

VMCA automatically manages and replaces certificates for ESXi hosts by default. This approach simplifies certificate management in environments that do not require external CA integration.

b. Custom CA-Signed Certificates for ESXi:

For enhanced security, custom CA-signed certificates can be used to replace the default VMCA certificates. This involves generating a CSR from the ESXi host, submitting it to a CA, and replacing the host's certificates manually.

Steps to Replace ESXi Host Certificates:

- Generate CSR on the ESXi Host:

Log into the ESXi host using SSH and generate a CSR. Alternatively, you can use vCenter Server to manage this process.

- Submit CSR to a CA:

Submit the CSR to an external CA and obtain the signed certificate and the corresponding private key.

- Replace the Host Certificate:

Replace the existing VMCA-signed certificate with the custom CA-signed certificate using vSphere Client or manually via SSH.

3. Renewing Certificates

SSL certificates have an expiration date, and renewing them in a timely manner is essential to avoid service disruptions. Both VMCA-signed and CA-signed certificates need to be tracked for expiration.

a. VMCA-Signed Certificate Renewal:

VMCA automatically renews certificates for vCenter Server and ESXi hosts before they expire, reducing administrative overhead. However, administrators can manually trigger the renewal process if needed.

b. CA-Signed Certificate Renewal:

Certificates signed by an external CA need to be renewed manually. The process involves generating a new CSR, submitting it to the CA for renewal, and replacing the old certificate with the new one.

4. Managing Certificate Authority Integration

For organizations that require external CA integration, setting up a Certificate Authority infrastructure is necessary. External CAs, such as Microsoft CA or Entrust, provide a higher level of trust for SSL certificates in environments where certificates are used for public-facing services or require compliance with strict regulations.

Steps for Integrating with an External CA:

- Install Root Certificates:

Install the external CA's root certificate on vCenter Server and ESXi hosts to establish trust for custom CA-signed certificates.

- Configure Certificate Manager:

Use the vCenter Server Certificate Manager to integrate the external CA and automate the CSR generation and certificate replacement process.

- Monitor Expiration Dates:

Set up monitoring for certificate expiration and automate reminders or renewal requests to avoid service outages caused by expired certificates.

Troubleshooting Common Certificate Issues

Expired Certificates:

One of the most common issues in vSphere environments is expired certificates. If an SSL certificate expires, communication between vCenter, ESXi hosts, and clients may fail. Ensure that expiration dates are monitored and renew certificates well in advance.

SSL Handshake Errors:

These errors occur when there's a mismatch between the certificate presented by a component and what is trusted by the client or server. This can happen if the root certificate is missing or if there's a misconfiguration in the certificate chain.

Incorrect Certificate Installation:

If certificates are not installed correctly or the private key does not match the certificate, vSphere services may fail to start. Ensure that both the certificate and corresponding private key are uploaded correctly during the replacement process.

Best Practices for Managing Certificates

Automate Certificate Management:

Use the vCenter Server Certificate Manager to automate the generation, installation, and renewal of SSL certificates. Automation reduces the risk of manual errors and simplifies the process.

Monitor Certificate Expiry:

Set up automated alerts to monitor certificate expiration dates. This ensures that certificates are renewed before they expire, preventing service disruptions.

Use a Trusted CA:

For environments requiring enhanced security or public trust, use certificates signed by a trusted external CA. This is especially important for environments that need to meet regulatory compliance.

Enable Certificate Revocation Checking:

Enable certificate revocation checking to ensure that revoked certificates are not trusted within the vSphere environment. This adds an extra layer of security in case a certificate is compromised.

EXAM-RELATED QUESTIONS ON SSL CERTIFICATE MANAGEMENT

For the VMware vSphere 8.x Professional certification exam, candidates should be prepared to answer questions about SSL certificate management, including:

How do you replace VMCA-signed certificates with certificates from an external CA?

➢ Be prepared to describe the steps for generating a CSR, submitting it to a CA, and replacing certificates in vCenter Server and ESXi hosts.

What tools are available for managing certificates in vSphere?

➢ Understand how to use the vCenter Server Certificate Manager and vSphere Client to manage SSL certificates, renewals, and replacements.

How does VMware Trust Authority integrate with certificate management?

➢ Expect questions on how certificates are used in conjunction with VMware Trust Authority for secure communications and trusted infrastructure.

P.S.

Practicing SSL certificate management in a lab environment is crucial for mastering these concepts. Familiarizing yourself with vSphere's certificate management tools and workflows will help you confidently handle certificate-related tasks in both real-world deployments and the certification exam.

VSPHERE REPLICATION AND DISASTER RECOVERY CONCEPTS

vSphere Replication is a key component of VMware's disaster recovery strategy, providing asynchronous replication of virtual machines (VMs) to ensure data protection and availability across multiple sites. It enables the replication of VMs between hosts, clusters, and even different vSphere environments, facilitating disaster recovery by allowing organizations to recover critical workloads in the event of site failures, data corruption, or other disasters. This section will explain the core concepts of vSphere Replication, including Recovery Point Objective (RPO) and Recovery Time Objective (RTO), and cover how to configure and manage vSphere Replication in a multi-site environment. Real-world disaster recovery scenarios will also be discussed, alongside tips for exam preparation.

Key Disaster Recovery Concepts: RPO and RTO

Before diving into the details of vSphere Replication, it is essential to understand two fundamental disaster recovery metrics: Recovery Point Objective (RPO) and Recovery Time Objective (RTO).

Recovery Point Objective (RPO):

The RPO defines the maximum acceptable amount of data loss in the event of a disaster. It is typically measured in minutes or hours and indicates how often replication occurs. For example, if an organization has an RPO of 4 hours, it means that in the event of a disaster, up to 4 hours of data might be lost, as that is the interval between replication operations. vSphere Replication allows RPO to be configured as low as 5 minutes or as high as 24 hours, providing flexibility based on workload criticality.

Recovery Time Objective (RTO):

The RTO refers to the maximum amount of time it should take to restore services and recover from a disaster. It reflects the organization's tolerance for downtime. A low RTO ensures that workloads are recovered quickly, minimizing the impact of an outage on business operations. The efficiency of the failover process and the speed with which replicated data is brought online contribute to meeting RTO targets.

Both RPO and RTO are critical to defining the overall disaster recovery (DR) strategy for an organization, as they directly influence how often replication should occur and how quickly services can be restored in the event of a failure.

What is vSphere Replication?

vSphere Replication is VMware's native hypervisor-based replication solution designed to protect VMs and ensure availability in case of site failures or disasters. Unlike storage-based replication solutions, vSphere Replication operates at the VM level, making it more flexible and granular. It replicates only the VM changes (rather than entire VMs) to minimize bandwidth usage and reduce the amount of time it takes to replicate data.

Key Features of vSphere Replication:

Hypervisor-Level Replication:

vSphere Replication replicates VMs at the hypervisor level, providing flexibility to replicate between different storage arrays and infrastructure setups.

Asynchronous Replication:

vSphere Replication is asynchronous, meaning that data is replicated at intervals based on the configured RPO. This allows for greater flexibility and less impact on bandwidth than synchronous replication.

Flexible RPO Settings:

Administrators can configure different RPO settings for different VMs, allowing critical workloads to be replicated more frequently than less critical workloads.

Multi-Site Replication:

vSphere Replication supports multi-site environments, enabling replication between different physical sites or data centers, providing protection against site-wide disasters.

Integration with VMware Site Recovery Manager (SRM):

vSphere Replication integrates with VMware Site Recovery Manager (SRM), a disaster recovery orchestration tool that automates failover and failback processes, making disaster recovery more efficient and streamlined.

Configuring vSphere Replication

Step 1: Install vSphere Replication

To set up vSphere Replication, administrators must deploy the vSphere Replication Appliance in their vSphere environment. This appliance provides the necessary services for managing replication tasks and integrates with vCenter Server.

Steps to install the vSphere Replication Appliance:

- Download the vSphere Replication Appliance from the VMware portal.
- Deploy the appliance as an OVF template in the vSphere environment.
- Configure the IP address and network settings for the appliance.
- Connect the appliance to vCenter Server, ensuring that vCenter can communicate with the replication services.

Step 2: Configure Replication for VMs

Once the vSphere Replication Appliance is deployed, replication can be configured at the VM level. Each VM can be configured to replicate to a secondary site or location, based on the defined RPO.

Steps to configure VM replication:

- In the vSphere Client, select the VM to be replicated.
- Right-click the VM and choose Configure Replication.
- Select the target location (either a different host, cluster, or vSphere environment).
- Define the RPO based on how frequently the VM should be replicated. The RPO can be set anywhere between 5 minutes and 24 hours.
- Optionally, enable network compression to optimize bandwidth usage during replication.
- Configure the quiescing options, which ensures the consistency of VM data by pausing the VM's filesystem during replication.

Step 3: Monitor Replication and Recovery

After configuring replication, vSphere Replication continuously monitors the VM and replicates data based on the defined RPO. In case of a disaster, the replicated VM can be recovered at the secondary site.

Steps to recover a VM:

- In the event of a failure at the primary site, go to the vSphere Client at the secondary site.
- Access the vSphere Replication Appliance and select the VM to recover.
- Choose Recover, and vSphere Replication will bring the latest replicated VM data online at the secondary site, minimizing downtime and ensuring service availability.

Disaster Recovery Scenarios with vSphere Replication

Scenario 1: Multi-Site Disaster Recovery

- In a large enterprise, the primary data center experiences a power failure due to a natural disaster. The organization has configured vSphere Replication between their primary and secondary data centers.
- The replicated VMs in the secondary data center are brought online, using the last replicated data according to the configured RPO.
- Once the primary site is restored, the VMs are failed back from the secondary site to the primary site using vSphere Replication.

Scenario 2: Protecting Critical Workloads

- A business-critical database application is replicated with an RPO of 5 minutes to minimize data loss in case of failure.
- During a hardware failure on the ESXi host running the database VM, the replication ensures that the most recent data is available on the secondary site, enabling the database to be recovered quickly with minimal data loss.

Best Practices for Using vSphere Replication

Prioritize Critical Workloads:

Configure different RPOs based on the criticality of each workload. Critical applications should have more frequent replication intervals to minimize data loss.

Test Recovery Plans Regularly:

Regularly test your disaster recovery plans by simulating failover scenarios. This ensures that the organization is prepared to respond effectively in the event of a real disaster.

Monitor Replication Health:

Use the vSphere Client or vRealize Operations Manager to monitor replication status and health. Ensure that replication is running as expected and that there are no issues with data integrity.

Optimize Network Usage:

Enable compression and network optimization options to reduce bandwidth usage during replication, especially in bandwidth-constrained environments.

EXAM PREPARATION TIPS FOR VSPHERE REPLICATION

When preparing for the VMware vSphere 8.x Professional certification exam, candidates should be familiar with the following topics related to vSphere Replication:

➢ **Understanding RPO and RTO:** Be prepared to explain how different RPOs impact replication frequency and how RTO affects recovery time in disaster recovery scenarios.

➢ **Configuring vSphere Replication:** Know the steps required to install the vSphere Replication Appliance and configure replication for VMs.

➢ **Disaster Recovery Scenarios:** Be able to describe how vSphere Replication can be used in multi-site recovery, failover, and failback scenarios.

➢ **Integrating with VMware SRM:** Understand how VMware Site Recovery Manager (SRM) integrates with vSphere Replication to automate disaster recovery processes.

P.S.

Practicing vSphere Replication in a lab environment will help solidify these concepts and ensure you are well-prepared for both real-world disaster recovery management and exam scenarios.

Backup Strategies and File-Based Backups in VMware vSphere 8.x

In any IT environment, backups are essential to ensure the continuity of business operations and the integrity of data. VMware vSphere 8.x provides various options for protecting virtual infrastructure through efficient backup strategies. Backups in vSphere environments must account for the unique aspects of virtualized workloads, including multiple virtual machines (VMs) on a single host, dynamic resource allocation, and storage efficiency. This section will focus on file-based backups, different backup methods, and the best practices for ensuring data integrity. Additionally, we will explore how to configure file-based backups in vCenter Server and offer tips on preparing for exam questions on backup management.

The Importance of Backups in Virtual Environments

In virtual environments, backups protect against data loss caused by hardware failures, software corruption, security breaches, or accidental deletions. Without proper backup solutions, organizations risk losing critical workloads and data, resulting in downtime, loss of productivity, and potential financial loss.

VMware vSphere environments introduce several challenges that make backup strategies more complex compared to traditional physical infrastructure:

➢ **Density of VMs:** Multiple VMs can reside on a single host, so backing up an entire host or datastore means capturing numerous VMs with varying configurations and workloads.
➢ **Dynamic Resource Allocation:** Virtual environments allow resources like CPU and memory to be allocated dynamically, which may complicate traditional backup methods.
➢ **Efficient Storage:** Backups must be space-efficient, avoiding redundant storage while ensuring rapid recovery in the event of a disaster.

Backup Methods in VMware vSphere

VMware vSphere supports several backup methods, each suitable for different recovery point objectives (RPO) and recovery time objectives (RTO):

a. Full VM Backups:

Full VM backups capture the entire state of a VM, including its configuration, virtual disk files, and system memory. This method ensures that a complete copy of the VM can be restored. However, full VM backups require substantial storage space and can take longer to perform.

b. Incremental and Differential Backups:

Incremental backups store only the data that has changed since the last backup, while differential backups capture all changes made since the last full backup. Both methods are more storage-efficient than full VM backups and reduce backup time, but they require careful management to ensure a smooth recovery process.

c. File-Based Backups:

File-based backups focus on backing up specific files or folders within a VM or vCenter Server itself. This method is efficient in cases where only critical files need protection. File-based backups are particularly useful for vCenter Server Appliance (VCSA), where backing up critical configuration and database files ensures that the vCenter Server instance can be quickly restored.

d. Snapshot-Based Backups:

Snapshots capture the state of a VM at a specific point in time, including its memory and disk contents. While snapshots are useful for short-term recovery scenarios, they are not ideal for long-term backups due to the performance overhead they introduce.

File-Based Backups in VMware vSphere

In vSphere 8.x, file-based backups are a key feature for protecting the vCenter Server Appliance (VCSA). These backups capture critical components, such as the vCenter Server configuration, inventory, and database, ensuring that vCenter can be restored quickly in case of a failure.

Configuring File-Based Backups in vCenter Server

File-based backups for vCenter Server can be scheduled and configured through the vSphere Client. The following steps outline the process for setting up a file-based backup in vCenter:

➢ Access the vSphere Client:

Log into the vSphere Client and navigate to the vCenter Server instance that you wish to back up.

➢ Open the Backup Configuration:

Go to the Administration tab in vSphere Client and click on Backup under the Backup & Restore section. This will open the configuration interface for file-based backups.

➢ **Configure Backup Location:**

Specify the backup target (the location where the backup will be stored). The target can be an FTP, SFTP, HTTP, HTTPS, or NFS server. Ensure that the location is secure and has sufficient storage to accommodate the backup files.

➢ **Schedule Backups:**

Set up a backup schedule to automate backups at regular intervals. The frequency of the backups should align with your organization's RPO and RTO. Critical systems may require daily backups, while less critical systems can be backed up weekly.

➢ **Configure Retention Policies:**

Define retention policies for the backup files, specifying how long backups should be kept before being deleted. This helps manage storage usage and ensures compliance with data retention regulations.

➢ **Initiate Manual Backups:**

While automated backups are crucial, you can also initiate a manual backup at any time from the Backup tab. This is useful when making major changes to vCenter Server or before performing significant upgrades.

➢ **Test Restore Functionality:**

After configuring backups, periodically test the restore process to ensure that the backups are functional and can be used to recover the vCenter Server instance. Testing restores is a best practice that ensures the reliability of the backup solution.

Restoring from File-Based Backups

Restoring vCenter Server from a file-based backup is straightforward and can be done using the vCenter Server Management Interface (VAMI). To perform a restore:

- Access the VAMI by navigating to the vCenter Server Appliance management URL (e.g., https://<VCSA_IP>:5480).
- Choose the Restore option and specify the location of the backup files.
- Select the backup file you want to restore and follow the prompts to complete the restoration process.

- File-based backups can be restored to the same vCenter Server instance or a new instance if the original appliance is no longer available.

Best Practices for Backup Management

Align Backups with Business Needs:

Backup schedules and retention policies should be aligned with the criticality of the workloads being protected. For example, critical VMs should have more frequent backups with longer retention periods.

Off-Site Backup Storage:

Store backups in a secure, off-site location to ensure that they are accessible even if the primary data center is compromised. This also protects against ransomware attacks or hardware failures.

Test Backup and Recovery Procedures:

Regularly test the backup and recovery processes to ensure that they work as expected. Performing test recoveries verifies the integrity of backup files and helps avoid surprises during an actual recovery scenario.

Monitor Backup Health:

Use vRealize Operations or other monitoring tools to track the status of backups. Alerts can be configured to notify administrators if a backup fails, ensuring that issues are addressed promptly.

Document Backup Configurations:

Maintain detailed documentation of the backup configuration, including schedules, retention policies, and recovery procedures. This documentation will help in troubleshooting issues and ensuring consistent management of backups across the environment.

EXAM TIPS ON BACKUP MANAGEMENT AND RECOVERY

For the VMware vSphere 8.x Professional certification exam, candidates should focus on the following areas related to backup strategies:

➢ **Understanding Backup Types:** Be prepared to explain the differences between full VM backups, incremental/differential backups, file-based backups, and snapshots.

➢ **Configuring File-Based Backups:** Know the steps involved in configuring file-based backups for vCenter Server Appliance (VCSA) and how to restore from those backups.

➢ **Best Practices:** Be familiar with industry best practices for data integrity, such as testing restores, configuring backup schedules, and ensuring off-site backup storage.

➢ **Backup and Recovery Scenarios:** Expect questions that involve backup management in disaster recovery scenarios, including how to recover critical services from backups.

P.S.

Hands-on practice with vSphere backup and recovery configurations is essential for mastering these topics and successfully answering exam questions. Using a lab environment to configure file-based backups and simulate recovery scenarios will deepen your understanding of backup management in vSphere.

Configuring VMware Site Recovery Manager (SRM)

VMware Site Recovery Manager (SRM) is an advanced disaster recovery (DR) solution that automates the orchestration of failover and failback processes in VMware environments. SRM integrates seamlessly with vSphere Replication and storage-based replication solutions to ensure the protection and recovery of virtualized workloads across different sites. By automating the disaster recovery process, SRM minimizes downtime, reduces human error, and provides organizations with confidence in their ability to recover from site failures.

In this section, we will cover how SRM works, the steps to configure it, how to set up recovery plans, and best practices for testing disaster recovery scenarios. Additionally, we will provide exam tips for mastering SRM configurations and troubleshooting in the VMware vSphere 8.x Professional certification.

Role of VMware Site Recovery Manager (SRM) in Disaster Recovery

SRM is designed to manage the disaster recovery process by automating the failover and failback of virtual machines (VMs) between two or more sites. In disaster recovery, failover refers to the process of transferring workloads from a primary site to a secondary site when the primary site becomes unavailable due to an outage or failure. Failback is the process of returning workloads from the secondary site back to the primary site once the issue is resolved.

Key benefits of SRM include:

Automated Failover and Failback: SRM automates the complex tasks of shutting down VMs at the primary site, powering them on at the secondary site, and reconfiguring networking and storage. This reduces the time needed to recover operations.

Recovery Plans: SRM allows administrators to create and customize recovery plans that specify the order in which VMs should be recovered and define other configuration details such as IP address changes or boot priorities.

Non-Disruptive Testing: One of SRM's most powerful features is the ability to test recovery plans in an isolated environment without affecting production workloads. This allows organizations to verify their DR readiness regularly.

Integration with vSphere Replication

SRM integrates with vSphere Replication, VMware's native hypervisor-based replication tool, to replicate VMs between sites. vSphere Replication provides asynchronous replication of VM data at the hypervisor level, enabling data to be replicated to a secondary site with configurable Recovery Point Objectives (RPO) as low as 5 minutes.

When SRM is integrated with vSphere Replication:

vSphere Replication handles the continuous replication of VM data between the primary and secondary sites.

SRM manages the failover and recovery process, ensuring that replicated VMs can be recovered according to predefined recovery plans.

In addition to vSphere Replication, SRM can also integrate with array-based replication solutions provided by third-party storage vendors, offering a high level of flexibility for different storage environments.

Steps to Configure VMware Site Recovery Manager (SRM)

Step 1: Install and Configure SRM

To configure SRM, you need to install the SRM Server at both the protected (primary) site and the recovery (secondary) site. Each site's SRM Server instance will communicate with the other, ensuring coordination between the two locations during the disaster recovery process.

Install SRM at the Primary Site:

- Download the SRM software from the VMware Customer Connect portal and install it on a supported Windows Server.
- During installation, connect SRM to the vCenter Server instance at the primary site.
- After installation, configure the Site Pairing by linking the primary SRM instance to the SRM instance at the recovery site.

Install SRM at the Recovery Site:

- Repeat the installation process for the secondary site, ensuring that it connects to the vCenter Server at the recovery site.
- Complete the site pairing by establishing communication between the SRM instances at both sites.

Step 2: Configure vSphere Replication or Array-Based Replication

If you are using vSphere Replication, follow these steps to configure replication between the two sites:

- Deploy the vSphere Replication Appliance at both the primary and secondary sites.
- Configure VM replication by selecting the VMs to be replicated and defining the target site (secondary site) and RPO settings.
- Ensure that the replication health is monitored in the vSphere Client to verify that the VMs are being replicated correctly.
- For array-based replication, you will need to configure replication at the storage level using the vendor's array management tools, and SRM will integrate with these tools to manage the recovery.

Step 3: Create and Configure Recovery Plans

Once replication is configured, you can set up Recovery Plans in SRM. A recovery plan defines the steps that SRM will take to fail over VMs from the primary site to the secondary site in the event of a disaster.

Create Protection Groups:

A Protection Group is a collection of VMs that are protected by SRM. Protection groups are used to group related VMs that need to fail over together. For example, you might create a protection group for your production web servers and another for your database servers.

Protection groups are associated with the replicated VMs configured in vSphere Replication or array-based replication.

Set Up Recovery Plans:

- In SRM, create a Recovery Plan and assign protection groups to it.
- Define the priority order in which VMs should be recovered. For example, you may want critical infrastructure services (e.g., DNS, Active Directory) to be recovered before application servers.
- Specify additional actions such as IP address changes, network reconfiguration, or script execution to adapt VMs to the new site's network and infrastructure.

Step 4: Test Recovery Plans

A key feature of SRM is the ability to test recovery plans without impacting production environments. Testing ensures that the disaster recovery strategy is effective and identifies any configuration issues that need to be addressed.

To test a recovery plan:

- In the SRM UI, select the recovery plan to be tested.
- Choose the Test Recovery Plan option. SRM will initiate the failover process in an isolated environment, ensuring that the test does not affect live production workloads.
- SRM will bring up the VMs at the secondary site in a test network to simulate the recovery process.
- After testing, review the results and resolve any issues identified during the test.

Step 5: Execute Failover and Failback

In the event of a disaster, SRM automates the failover process by:

- Shutting down VMs at the primary site.
- Powering on replicated VMs at the recovery site.
- Reconfiguring networking to ensure that the VMs function correctly in the new environment.
- Once the primary site is restored, you can execute the failback process using SRM, which reverses the replication and migrates the VMs back to the primary site.

EXAM TIPS FOR VMWARE SRM

For the VMware vSphere 8.x Professional certification exam, it's important to have a solid understanding of SRM concepts and configurations. Here are key topics to focus on:

- **Site Pairing and SRM Installation:** Be familiar with the process of installing SRM at both the primary and recovery sites, as well as the steps to establish site pairing.

- **Recovery Plans and Protection Groups:** Understand how to create protection groups, set recovery priorities, and configure recovery plans based on business needs.

- **Testing Recovery Plans:** Know how to perform non-disruptive tests of recovery plans to verify disaster recovery readiness.

- **Integration with vSphere Replication:** Be prepared to explain how SRM integrates with vSphere Replication and other storage-based replication technologies.

- **Troubleshooting:** Expect questions on how to troubleshoot common SRM issues, such as replication failures or problems during the recovery process.

P.S.

Hands-on practice with SRM in a test environment is essential for mastering the concepts and configurations related to disaster recovery. Regularly test recovery plans in SRM to ensure you're fully prepared for both real-world scenarios and exam questions.

Overview of Vsphere with Tanzu

vSphere with Tanzu is VMware's powerful solution that integrates Kubernetes directly into vSphere environments, transforming VMware's flagship virtualization platform into a robust infrastructure for both virtual machines (VMs) and containers. As organizations increasingly adopt cloud-native and DevOps practices, vSphere with Tanzu enables IT teams to seamlessly manage traditional applications alongside modern containerized applications, all within the same infrastructure. This integration simplifies operations, reduces overhead, and accelerates the transition to a modern, container-based approach without the need for a separate platform to manage Kubernetes clusters.

In this section, we'll explore how vSphere with Tanzu works, its role in modern IT infrastructures, the benefits it provides to cloud-native and DevOps environments, and the key concepts to focus on for the VMware vSphere 8.x Professional certification exam.

What is vSphere with Tanzu?

vSphere with Tanzu is VMware's implementation of Kubernetes built directly into the vSphere platform, allowing administrators to deploy and manage Kubernetes clusters natively within vSphere. This solution bridges the gap between traditional VM-based workloads and containerized workloads by unifying their management into a single platform.

At its core, vSphere with Tanzu transforms vSphere into a platform capable of managing both:

Virtual Machines (VMs): Traditional, legacy applications that require VM-based infrastructure.

Containers: Modern, cloud-native applications that utilize Kubernetes for container orchestration.

With vSphere with Tanzu, IT operations teams can leverage the existing infrastructure and tools they are familiar with, while developers can deploy their Kubernetes workloads using standard tools and APIs. This dual-purpose functionality allows organizations to run VMs and containers side by side, providing flexibility and future-proofing the infrastructure for new cloud-native technologies.

Key Components of vSphere with Tanzu

vSphere Pods:

vSphere with Tanzu introduces the concept of vSphere Pods, which are native Kubernetes pods that run directly on the ESXi hypervisor. These pods are isolated from each other at the VM level, offering the same level of security and performance that VMs receive, but for containerized workloads. This enables organizations to deploy Kubernetes workloads with the same benefits that vSphere provides for VMs, such as security, networking, and resource management.

Supervisor Cluster:

The Supervisor Cluster is a core component of vSphere with Tanzu. It transforms ESXi hosts into Kubernetes worker nodes. By running Kubernetes directly on the ESXi hypervisor, the Supervisor Cluster allows vSphere administrators to manage Kubernetes clusters natively. The Supervisor Cluster is responsible for creating Namespaces, which are virtual boundaries that isolate resources such as compute, storage, and networking for Kubernetes workloads.

Tanzu Kubernetes Grid (TKG):

Tanzu Kubernetes Grid (TKG) is VMware's enterprise Kubernetes runtime that is fully integrated into vSphere with Tanzu. It enables the deployment of fully functional Kubernetes clusters on vSphere infrastructure. TKG provides a consistent Kubernetes experience across private and public cloud environments, ensuring that organizations can manage Kubernetes clusters at scale, whether in an on-premises data center or in the cloud.

Namespaces:

Namespaces in vSphere with Tanzu allow IT teams to allocate resources (compute, storage, networking) for Kubernetes workloads. A Namespace functions as a resource boundary within a Supervisor Cluster and enables role-based access control (RBAC) and quota management. Developers can request access to these resources to deploy and manage Kubernetes workloads, making it easier to organize, manage, and allocate resources for different teams and projects.

Benefits of vSphere with Tanzu in Cloud-Native and DevOps Environments

The integration of Kubernetes into the vSphere ecosystem provides several key benefits, particularly for organizations embracing cloud-native applications and DevOps practices.

1. Simplified Kubernetes Management

One of the biggest challenges for organizations adopting Kubernetes is managing the infrastructure. With vSphere with Tanzu, Kubernetes is embedded directly into vSphere, making it easier for administrators to manage both VMs and containers from a single platform. This eliminates the need for a separate Kubernetes management platform, reducing complexity and operational overhead.

2. Unified Infrastructure for VMs and Containers

In traditional environments, VMs and containers often run on separate infrastructures, each with its own management tools and workflows. vSphere with Tanzu unifies these infrastructures, allowing organizations to run both VMs and containers on the same ESXi hypervisor. This results in more efficient resource utilization, simplifies operations, and allows IT teams to use existing skills and tools to manage containers alongside VMs.

3. Flexibility for Developers and IT Operations

For organizations adopting DevOps practices, vSphere with Tanzu provides the flexibility needed to support both traditional and modern workloads. Developers can work with Kubernetes APIs and deploy containerized applications using the tools they are familiar with, while IT operations teams maintain control over infrastructure using the same tools and policies they use to manage VMs.

4. Enhanced Security and Compliance

Security and compliance are major concerns when deploying containerized workloads, especially in production environments. vSphere with Tanzu provides robust security features, such as isolation between workloads (using vSphere Pods) and role-based access control (RBAC) within Namespaces. This allows organizations to maintain a secure environment while benefiting from the agility of Kubernetes.

5. Seamless Integration with Tanzu Kubernetes Grid

Tanzu Kubernetes Grid (TKG) integrates seamlessly with vSphere with Tanzu, providing a consistent Kubernetes experience across on-premises and cloud environments. This enables organizations to deploy multi-cloud Kubernetes clusters, ensuring portability and consistency across hybrid environments.

Configuring and Managing vSphere with Tanzu

Step 1: Enable vSphere with Tanzu

To configure vSphere with Tanzu, you must first enable vSphere with Tanzu in your vCenter Server environment. This involves deploying a Supervisor Cluster on a set of ESXi hosts, which transforms the hosts into Kubernetes worker nodes.

Prepare the Environment:

Ensure that the ESXi hosts are part of a vSphere cluster and that the required networking (e.g., NSX-T or vSphere networking) is configured to support Kubernetes workloads.

Enable the Supervisor Cluster:

- In vSphere Client, navigate to Workload Management and select the vSphere cluster where you want to deploy the Supervisor Cluster.
- Follow the prompts to enable the Supervisor Cluster, which transforms the ESXi hosts into Kubernetes worker nodes.

Step 2: Create and Manage Namespaces

Once the Supervisor Cluster is enabled, you can create Namespaces to allocate resources for Kubernetes workloads. Each Namespace is isolated and allows developers to deploy containerized applications securely.

Create a Namespace:

- In vSphere Client, go to Workload Management and create a new Namespace within the Supervisor Cluster.
- Assign compute, storage, and networking resources to the Namespace.

Assign Permissions:

Configure role-based access control (RBAC) for the Namespace by assigning users or groups with specific roles (e.g., Developer, Admin) to manage the workloads within the Namespace.

Step 3: Deploy Kubernetes Workloads

With the Supervisor Cluster and Namespaces configured, developers can now deploy Kubernetes workloads using familiar Kubernetes tools like kubectl. Developers can interact with the Supervisor Cluster or deploy Tanzu Kubernetes clusters (TKGs) to run their containerized applications.

EXAM-FOCUSED CONTENT ON VSPHERE WITH TANZU

For the VMware vSphere 8.x Professional certification exam, there are several key topics to focus on related to vSphere with Tanzu:

➤ Enabling vSphere with Tanzu:

Understand the steps required to enable vSphere with Tanzu in a vCenter Server environment and the prerequisites, such as networking (NSX-T or vSphere networking).

➤ Supervisor Cluster and Namespaces:

Be familiar with the role of the Supervisor Cluster and Namespaces in managing Kubernetes workloads. You should understand how to create and configure Namespaces and allocate resources.

➤ vSphere Pods and Kubernetes Integration:

Know the differences between vSphere Pods and traditional Kubernetes pods, and how Tanzu Kubernetes Grid (TKG) integrates with vSphere with Tanzu to manage Kubernetes clusters.

➤ Managing VMs and Containers:

Understand how vSphere with Tanzu allows organizations to manage both VMs and containers from a single platform and the benefits this provides for DevOps and cloud-native environments.

P.S.

Hands-on practice with vSphere with Tanzu is critical for mastering these concepts. Set up a lab environment to practice enabling Tanzu, creating Supervisor Clusters, and deploying Kubernetes workloads to ensure you are fully prepared for both real-world scenarios and exam questions.

INTRODUCTION TO VMWARE POWERCLI

VMware PowerCLI is a powerful command-line interface tool designed to automate the management and configuration of VMware vSphere environments. It is a set of PowerShell modules built specifically for vSphere that allow administrators to automate routine tasks, manage infrastructure, and streamline operations efficiently. By using PowerCLI, administrators can script complex processes, eliminate repetitive manual tasks, and ensure consistent configuration management across large-scale virtualized environments.

This section will introduce you to the basics of PowerCLI, how it helps with automation, and some key commands and scripts for managing virtual machines (VMs), resources, and monitoring tasks. We'll also cover real-world use cases, exam tips, and guidance on how to use PowerCLI effectively.

What is VMware PowerCLI?

VMware PowerCLI is a collection of PowerShell modules that provide cmdlets for managing VMware infrastructure directly from a command-line interface. These cmdlets allow administrators to perform various tasks in vSphere environments, including provisioning, configuration, monitoring, and automation of VMs, hosts, storage, and networks.

PowerCLI is built on Microsoft PowerShell, making it accessible to anyone familiar with PowerShell scripting. It simplifies complex tasks by allowing administrators to manage resources with commands or scripts rather than using the vSphere Client GUI. PowerCLI helps boost efficiency, especially in large-scale deployments or when administrators need to perform bulk operations.

Why Use PowerCLI for Automation?

a. Automation of Routine Tasks:

PowerCLI is ideal for automating repetitive tasks, such as creating or modifying multiple VMs, managing storage, or configuring networking for hosts. It reduces the need for manual intervention and saves time, particularly in environments with many VMs or hosts.

b. Consistency Across Environments:

Automation ensures that tasks are completed the same way every time, which helps maintain consistency in configuration, security, and management practices across different environments.

c. Scalability:

In large vSphere environments, where managing hundreds or thousands of VMs manually would be impractical, PowerCLI scripts can scale operations across multiple VMs or hosts simultaneously, making it easier to manage at scale.

d. Flexibility and Customization:

PowerCLI scripts can be customized to meet specific business or technical requirements. It also integrates well with other IT automation tools and scripts, providing flexibility in complex workflows.

e. Efficient Reporting and Monitoring:

Administrators can use PowerCLI to gather detailed information about the state of their virtual infrastructure, generate reports, and automate monitoring processes.

Basic Commands and Scripts in PowerCLI

PowerCLI provides a broad range of cmdlets that can be used to automate tasks such as VM creation, resource allocation, and environment monitoring. Below are some common PowerCLI commands and examples of how to use them in scripts:

1. Connecting to a vCenter Server

Before executing any commands, you must first establish a connection to the vCenter Server or ESXi host. The Connect-VIServer cmdlet is used for this purpose:

```powershell
Connect-VIServer -Server <vcenter-server-name> -User <username> -Password <password>
```

Example:

```powershell
Connect-VIServer -Server vc.example.com -User admin -Password "password123"
```

This command establishes a connection to the vCenter Server, allowing you to execute further PowerCLI commands.

2. Creating a New Virtual Machine

Once connected to the vCenter Server, you can create a new VM using the New-VM cmdlet. This cmdlet allows you to specify various configuration options such as CPU, memory, and storage.

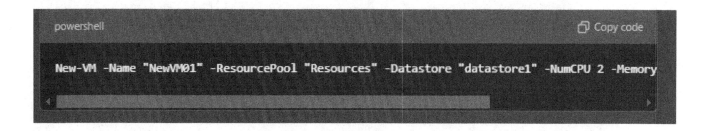

```powershell
New-VM -Name "NewVM01" -ResourcePool "Resources" -Datastore "datastore1" -NumCPU 2 -Memory
```

In this example:

A VM named NewVM01 is created.

It is allocated 2 CPUs and 4 GB of memory.

The VM is connected to datastore1 and the VM Network.

3. Modifying an Existing VM

You can modify the configuration of an existing VM using commands like Set-VM. For example, to change the CPU and memory configuration of a VM, you can run:

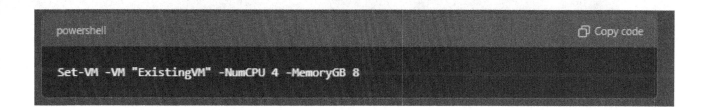

```powershell
Set-VM -VM "ExistingVM" -NumCPU 4 -MemoryGB 8
```

This command updates the specified VM to use 4 CPUs and 8 GB of memory.

4. Starting or Stopping VMs

Managing VM power states is another common task in vSphere environments. You can start, stop, or restart VMs using the following cmdlets:

- Start-VM to power on a VM:

```
Start-VM -VM "VMName"
```

- Stop-VM to power off a VM:

```
Stop-VM -VM "VMName" -Confirm:$false
```

- Restart-VM to reboot a VM:

```
Restart-VM -VM "VMName"
```

5. Managing Resources

You can also manage resources for VMs using PowerCLI. For example, to configure resource allocation for CPU and memory, you can use the following:

```
Set-VMResourceConfiguration -VM "VMName" -CpuReservationMHz 2000 -MemReservationMB 2048
```

This sets the CPU reservation to 2000 MHz and memory reservation to 2048 MB for the specified VM.

6. Monitoring VM Performance

PowerCLI also provides cmdlets to monitor the performance of VMs. The Get-Stat cmdlet is used to collect performance statistics from VMs, ESXi hosts, and other resources.

For example, to retrieve the CPU usage of a VM:

```
Get-Stat -Entity "VMName" -Stat cpu.usage.average -Start (Get-Date).AddHours(-1)
```

This command retrieves the average CPU usage of the VM in the last hour.

Real-World Use Cases for PowerCLI

➤ **Automated VM Provisioning:**

In environments where VMs need to be created frequently (e.g., development environments), PowerCLI can automate the provisioning of VMs with predefined configurations. This eliminates manual tasks and ensures consistent VM configurations across the infrastructure.

➤ **Bulk VM Configuration Changes:**

PowerCLI scripts are useful for making bulk configuration changes to multiple VMs at once, such as increasing memory, changing network settings, or migrating VMs to different datastores.

➤ **Scheduled Tasks and Maintenance:**

PowerCLI can be used to schedule routine tasks like VM backups, host patching, or performance monitoring. Automating these tasks ensures they are performed consistently without manual intervention.

➤ **Reporting and Compliance:**

Many organizations need regular reports on resource usage, VM performance, or compliance. PowerCLI can automate the generation of such reports, saving time and ensuring accuracy. For example, generating a report on all VMs' configurations or checking compliance against a baseline configuration can be done with a few lines of PowerCLI script.

EXAM TIPS FOR POWERCLI-RELATED TASKS

For the VMware vSphere 8.x Professional certification exam, candidates should have a solid understanding of PowerCLI commands and scripting for automating common vSphere tasks. Here are some key areas to focus on:

➤ **Basic PowerCLI Commands:**

Be familiar with the syntax and usage of core PowerCLI cmdlets such as New-VM, Set-VM, Start-VM, Stop-VM, Get-VM, and Get-Stat. Understand how to perform routine tasks such as creating VMs, managing resources, and monitoring performance.

➤ **Script Writing:**

Practice writing basic PowerCLI scripts to automate common tasks. You should be able to create scripts for bulk VM provisioning, resource management, and monitoring.

➤ **Integration with Other Automation Tools:**

Be aware of how PowerCLI can integrate with other tools, such as vRealize Orchestrator and PowerShell scripts, to build more comprehensive automation workflows.

➤ **Troubleshooting PowerCLI Issues:**

Be prepared to troubleshoot PowerCLI issues, such as connection problems with vCenter Server or ESXi hosts. Understanding how to handle common errors and exceptions in PowerCLI scripts is crucial.

➤ **Efficiency in Large Environments:**

Understand how to use PowerCLI to manage large-scale environments efficiently by using loops, filters, and pipelines to perform operations across many VMs or hosts simultaneously.

P.S.

Practicing PowerCLI commands in a test environment is essential for mastering automation tasks and configurations. Regularly working with scripts will help you gain the confidence needed for both the certification exam and real-world vSphere management scenarios.

Automating Tasks in vSphere

In VMware vSphere environments, automating common administrative tasks is essential for reducing manual workloads, improving consistency, and minimizing human error. By automating tasks like provisioning virtual machines (VMs), managing storage resources, and updating multiple hosts, administrators can ensure faster, more reliable operations. VMware PowerCLI and other VMware tools offer powerful capabilities to streamline these processes.

This section will cover how automation helps in day-to-day vSphere management, key use cases, and tips for mastering automation topics in the VMware vSphere 8.x Professional certification exam.

Why Automate vSphere Tasks?

In large-scale virtualized environments, manually managing infrastructure can be time-consuming and prone to errors. Automation addresses these issues by:

1. **Reducing Administrative Overhead:** Automation helps by offloading repetitive and time-consuming tasks from administrators. This allows them to focus on higher-value activities, such as optimizing performance and planning for future infrastructure needs.

2. **Improving Consistency:** Human errors are common in manual processes. Automating tasks ensures that configurations are applied consistently across all VMs, hosts, or clusters, improving overall stability and compliance.

3. **Scaling Operations:** In large environments, scaling operations manually can be daunting. Automation allows for seamless scaling across multiple hosts, VMs, or datastores without significant manual intervention.

Automating Common vSphere Tasks with PowerCLI

PowerCLI, a collection of PowerShell cmdlets for vSphere management, is one of the most commonly used tools for automating tasks in vSphere environments. It allows administrators to perform complex tasks with minimal effort by scripting actions that would otherwise require repetitive steps in the vSphere Client.

1. Automating VM Provisioning

Provisioning VMs manually for multiple users or workloads can be time-consuming, but PowerCLI can automate the entire process. Using the New-VM cmdlet, administrators can create VMs with predefined configurations (e.g., CPU, memory, datastore) through a simple script.

Example:

```powershell
New-VM -Name "TestVM" -ResourcePool "ClusterResources" -Datastore "datastore1" -NumCPU 2 -
```

This script creates a new VM called TestVM with 2 CPUs, 8 GB of RAM, and connects it to the specified network and datastore. Administrators can modify the script to deploy multiple VMs simultaneously, reducing the time it takes to configure each one manually.

2. Automating Storage Management

Automating storage tasks ensures that storage resources are properly allocated and monitored, especially in environments with multiple datastores. With PowerCLI, administrators can manage storage by provisioning new datastores, expanding existing ones, or moving VMs between datastores (also known as Storage vMotion).

Example:

```powershell
Move-VM -VM "VMName" -Datastore "NewDatastore"
```

This script moves the specified VM to a different datastore, automating what would typically require several manual steps in the vSphere Client.

3. Automating Host Updates

Keeping ESXi hosts up-to-date with the latest patches and firmware is critical for maintaining a secure and optimized environment. PowerCLI, in conjunction with VMware Update Manager (VUM), can automate the process of updating multiple hosts.

Example:

```powershell
Get-VMHost | Update-VMHost -Image "ESXi_7.0_Image" -Confirm:$false
```

This command retrieves a list of all ESXi hosts and applies the specified update image to each host automatically, reducing the need for manual updates across multiple hosts.

Other VMware Tools for Automation

While PowerCLI is one of the primary tools for automation, VMware offers other tools that can further enhance automation and orchestration:

1. VMware vRealize Orchestrator (vRO)

vRealize Orchestrator (vRO) is a powerful tool for automating complex workflows in VMware environments. It integrates with vSphere and other VMware products, allowing for cross-platform automation of both vSphere and non-vSphere tasks. Administrators can create complex workflows that automate tasks like user provisioning, storage management, or even external service integrations (e.g., integrating with cloud platforms).

2. VMware vRealize Automation (vRA)

vRealize Automation (vRA) extends automation capabilities beyond the virtualized infrastructure to provide Infrastructure-as-a-Service (IaaS) capabilities. With vRA, administrators can define blueprints for entire application stacks, including VMs, networks, and storage, and automate the deployment of these blueprints across multiple environments. vRA allows for policy-driven automation, improving governance and compliance.

Real-World Use Cases for Automation

a. Automating VM Lifecycle Management:

For environments where developers frequently request VMs for testing, automation can help streamline the entire VM lifecycle, from provisioning to decommissioning. Scripts can automate not only VM creation but also resource reclamation when VMs are no longer needed, ensuring that storage and compute resources are efficiently used.

b. Automating Datastore Monitoring and Alerting:

By using PowerCLI and vRO, administrators can automate datastore monitoring and create custom alerts. For example, a script can monitor datastore capacity and automatically trigger a notification when a datastore is approaching capacity, allowing administrators to proactively manage storage.

c. Automating ESXi Host Configuration:

For new ESXi hosts being added to a cluster, administrators can use PowerCLI scripts to automate host configuration. Scripts can be written to apply network configurations, attach datastores, and even configure the necessary security settings like lockdown mode.

TIPS FOR MASTERING AUTOMATION FOR THE EXAM

For the VMware vSphere 8.x Professional certification exam, automation is a critical area to master. Here are a few tips to help prepare:

➢ Learn Core PowerCLI Cmdlets:

Be familiar with common PowerCLI cmdlets such as New-VM, Set-VM, Move-VM, Start-VMHost, and Update-VMHost. Understanding these commands and their parameters will help you answer questions related to automating tasks in vSphere environments.

➢ Practice Scripting for Common Tasks:

Automating tasks such as VM creation, storage management, and host updates are likely to appear in exam questions. Practice writing scripts for these common tasks to ensure you are comfortable with the syntax and logic.

➢ **Understand vRealize Tools:**

While PowerCLI is the primary tool for automation, understanding the use cases for vRealize Orchestrator and vRealize Automation will give you a well-rounded view of VMware's automation ecosystem. Be familiar with basic concepts like workflow creation in vRO and blueprinting in vRA.

➢ **Troubleshoot Automation Issues:**

Be prepared to troubleshoot common automation issues, such as connection errors, incorrect parameters, or missing permissions. Understanding how to diagnose and resolve these problems is key for both real-world scenarios and exam questions.

➢ **Lab Practice:**

Set up a vSphere lab environment where you can practice running PowerCLI scripts and configuring automation workflows. Hands-on experience will be invaluable for both the exam and real-world applications.

P.S.

Hands-on practice with VMware automation tools will not only help you master exam topics but also equip you with the skills to efficiently manage large vSphere environments in your day-to-day work.

vSphere API and Automation Use Cases

The VMware vSphere API is a powerful tool that allows developers and administrators to programmatically interact with and manage vSphere environments. It provides a broad set of capabilities for integrating, automating, and extending the functionality of VMware infrastructure. By utilizing the vSphere API, organizations can automate complex operations, integrate vSphere with third-party tools, and build custom solutions to enhance the efficiency and scalability of their virtualized infrastructure.

In this section, we will explore the basics of the vSphere API, common automation use cases, and tips for preparing for vSphere API-focused exam questions.

What is the vSphere API?

The vSphere API is an interface that allows developers and IT administrators to interact programmatically with VMware's vSphere platform. It exposes the full range of functionality available in vSphere, from VM provisioning and configuration to storage management, performance monitoring, and even advanced features like Distributed Resource Scheduler (DRS) and vSphere High Availability (HA).

There are several flavors of APIs that VMware offers for different use cases:

vSphere Web Services API: Provides access to all the core features of vSphere via SOAP-based web services. It is widely used for automation and integration tasks.

vSphere Automation SDK: Supports REST APIs and is designed for developers looking for a more modern, lightweight interface to interact with vSphere.

vSphere API for Kubernetes (vSphere with Tanzu): Exposes Kubernetes-native constructs on vSphere, allowing for easier management of containerized applications within VMware environments.

The vSphere API allows for both read and write operations, meaning users can gather detailed information about their environment (e.g., resource usage, VM configurations) and also perform tasks such as creating VMs, managing networks, and deploying applications.

Use Cases for vSphere API Automation

The vSphere API is versatile and can be used in various automation scenarios. Here are some common automation tasks that organizations can perform using the vSphere API:

1. Automated Provisioning of VMs

One of the most frequent uses of the vSphere API is for automating the provisioning of virtual machines (VMs). Using the API, administrators can create VMs with specified configurations (CPU, memory, storage, and networking) and even clone VMs to create templates. This significantly reduces the time needed to deploy multiple VMs, making it particularly useful in development or testing environments.

Example: Using a REST API call to create a VM:

```
POST /rest/vcenter/vm
{
  "name": "NewVM",
  "guest_OS": "WINDOWS_9_64",
  "cpu": {
    "count": 2
  },
  "memory": {
    "size_MB": 4096
  }
}
```

This API request provisions a new Windows VM with 2 CPUs and 4 GB of memory.

2. Automating VM Lifecycle Management

VM lifecycle management can also be fully automated with the vSphere API. This includes tasks such as:

- Powering on or off VMs.
- Reconfiguring VM resources (e.g., increasing CPU or memory).
- Deleting VMs after they are no longer needed.
- By automating the lifecycle management of VMs, organizations can reduce operational overhead and ensure that resources are allocated dynamically based on workload demands.

3. Resource Monitoring and Capacity Management

The vSphere API can be used to automate resource monitoring and reporting. Developers can write scripts or applications that interact with the API to gather real-time data about resource usage, such as CPU and memory consumption, disk I/O, and network traffic. This data can be used to trigger automated actions, such as provisioning additional resources or migrating VMs when thresholds are exceeded.

Example: Using the API to query VM performance data (CPU usage, memory usage, etc.) and automatically scale up or down depending on the workload.

4. Automating Disaster Recovery Operations

The vSphere API also plays a critical role in disaster recovery scenarios. It can be integrated with disaster recovery tools like VMware Site Recovery Manager (SRM) to automate failover and failback processes. Organizations can programmatically manage DR configurations, create recovery plans, and even test failover processes through API calls.

5. Automating Snapshot Management

VM snapshots are an essential part of both backup strategies and test environments. Through the vSphere API, administrators can create, manage, and delete snapshots for VMs programmatically. This is particularly useful for automating periodic backups or creating snapshots before performing major updates on a VM.

Example: Create a snapshot using the vSphere REST API:

```
POST /rest/vcenter/vm/<vm-id>/snapshot
{
  "description": "Snapshot before update",
  "name": "PreUpdateSnapshot"
}
```

This creates a snapshot of a specified VM with a custom description and name.

6. Integration with Third-Party Tools

The vSphere API can be integrated with various third-party tools for monitoring, configuration management, and orchestration. For example, it can work alongside Ansible, Terraform, or Chef to automate the provisioning and configuration of VMs across a hybrid cloud environment. By leveraging the API, teams can ensure that their infrastructure is always in the desired state without manual intervention.

PREPARING FOR EXAM QUESTIONS ON VSPHERE API AUTOMATION

For the VMware vSphere 8.x Professional certification exam, understanding how to use the vSphere API in automation contexts is critical. Here are a few tips to help you prepare for API-based questions:

➢ **Familiarize Yourself with API Documentation:**

VMware provides detailed documentation for the vSphere API and vSphere Automation SDKs. Knowing where to find information on specific API calls and parameters is essential for the exam.

➢ **Understand REST vs. SOAP APIs:**

Be aware of the differences between the REST API (used for modern, lightweight automation tasks) and the SOAP-based Web Services API (used for more complex, traditional automation). You should be able to identify scenarios where one might be preferred over the other.

➢ **Learn Common API Calls:**

Practice writing or reviewing basic API calls for tasks such as VM provisioning, performance monitoring, and snapshot management. Understanding the structure of an API request (such as the method, endpoint, and body) will help you answer questions about API-based automation.

➢ **Automation Scenarios:**

Be prepared for exam scenarios that involve integrating the vSphere API with other automation tools, such as vRealize Orchestrator (vRO), Terraform, or Ansible. Knowing how the vSphere API interacts with these tools can help you solve real-world problems in the exam.

➢ **Scripting and Coding Skills:**

Having basic coding skills (especially in Python or PowerShell) will help you interact with the vSphere API more effectively. You don't need to be an expert developer, but understanding the syntax and how to make API calls programmatically is crucial.

P.S.

The vSphere API opens up a vast array of possibilities for automation and integration in VMware environments. From provisioning VMs to monitoring resource usage and managing disaster recovery processes, the API enables organizations to streamline and scale their operations. By mastering the vSphere API, administrators and developers can ensure their VMware infrastructure is optimized for both performance and efficiency.

Hands-on practice is key to mastering API-based automation. Consider setting up a lab environment where you can experiment with making API calls and integrating them into larger automation workflows. This experience will be invaluable for the exam and real-world applications.

SAMPLE QUESTIONS ON CORE VSPHERE CONCEPTS

When preparing for the VMware vSphere 8.x Professional certification exam, understanding core vSphere concepts is critical. The exam will test your knowledge of virtualization fundamentals, vSphere architecture, networking, and key operational tasks. In this section, we'll provide a range of sample questions—both multiple-choice and scenario-based—along with detailed explanations of the correct answers. These questions will help you gain insights into what to expect on the exam and guide you on how to approach similar questions effectively.

Question 1: Virtualization Fundamentals (Multiple Choice)

What is the primary benefit of virtualization in a vSphere environment?

    A) Increased physical hardware costs
    B) Improved application performance by directly accessing hardware
    C) Consolidation of workloads to maximize hardware resource utilization
    D) Increased management complexity

Correct Answer: C) Consolidation of workloads to maximize hardware resource utilization

Explanation:

The primary benefit of virtualization is the ability to consolidate multiple workloads (virtual machines) on a single physical host. This allows organizations to maximize hardware resource utilization, reduce hardware costs, and improve operational efficiency. Each VM can run its own operating system and applications, isolated from others, all while sharing the same underlying hardware. Virtualization improves flexibility, scalability, and reduces the physical hardware footprint, which is why it's widely used in vSphere environments.

Exam Tip: Questions like this test your understanding of the core principles of virtualization. Focus on the benefits such as reduced costs, improved resource efficiency, and flexibility.

Question 2: vSphere Architecture (Scenario-Based)

Scenario: You are managing a vSphere environment with multiple ESXi hosts. A new host is added to the cluster, but you receive a warning that the host is not connected to vCenter Server. You suspect that network connectivity is an issue.

What is the most likely cause of the connection issue, and how can you resolve it?

A) The host is not configured with the correct VLAN settings.
B) The host is running an incompatible version of ESXi.
C) The host's management network is down, and you need to restart the management agents.
D) The vCenter Server database is full, preventing the host from being added.

Correct Answer: C) The host's management network is down, and you need to restart the management agents.

Explanation:

The most common issue when a new ESXi host cannot connect to vCenter Server is a problem with the management network on the host. vCenter communicates with ESXi hosts through the management network, and if there are issues with the network configuration or the management agents, the host may appear as "disconnected." Restarting the management agents on the ESXi host often resolves this issue.

Command to restart management agents:

SSH into the host and run:

```shell
services.sh restart
```

his command restarts both the hostd and vpxa services, which are responsible for the communication between ESXi and vCenter Server.

Exam Tip: Scenario-based questions often test your ability to troubleshoot common issues in a vSphere environment. Pay attention to the details provided in the question, as they often contain clues about the underlying problem.

Question 3: Networking (Multiple Choice)

What is the purpose of a vSphere Distributed Switch (vDS)?

A) It provides centralized management for multiple ESXi hosts' networking configurations.
B) It enables VMs to communicate directly with each other, bypassing the ESXi host.
C) It simplifies physical switch configuration by automating VLAN creation.
D) It allows for independent virtual network adapters per VM.

Correct Answer: A) It provides centralized management for multiple ESXi hosts' networking configurations.

Explanation:

A vSphere Distributed Switch (vDS) provides a centralized way to manage and configure networking across multiple ESXi hosts. It allows you to define virtual networking policies at a cluster level, rather than configuring each host individually. With a vDS, network policies and configurations can be applied uniformly across all hosts, simplifying network management, especially in larger environments.

Exam Tip: Know the differences between Standard Switches (vSS) and Distributed Switches (vDS). vDS is more suitable for larger, more complex environments where consistent network policies are essential.

Question 4: Storage (Scenario-Based)

Scenario: A VM on an NFS datastore is showing degraded performance. Other VMs on the same datastore seem unaffected. What steps should you take to identify and resolve the performance issue?

A) Migrate the VM to a new datastore using Storage vMotion.
B) Increase the NFS server's memory allocation.
C) Check the NFS datastore latency using vSphere Performance Charts.
D) Increase the VM's memory allocation.

Correct Answer: C) Check the NFS datastore latency using vSphere Performance Charts.

Explanation:

When troubleshooting performance issues on a VM, checking storage latency is a critical first step. vSphere Performance Charts can show real-time and historical latency data for NFS datastores, helping you determine if there are any storage bottlenecks. Latency issues often indicate storage contention, I/O bottlenecks, or misconfigurations. If latency is unusually high, further investigation into the network connectivity to the NFS server or the performance of the NFS server itself is needed.

Exam Tip: Familiarize yourself with common performance monitoring tools in vSphere, such as vSphere Performance Charts and ESXTOP, to diagnose storage and network issues.

Question 5: High Availability (Multiple Choice)

In a vSphere High Availability (HA) cluster, what happens when an ESXi host fails?

- A) All VMs on the host are permanently shut down.
- B) HA automatically restarts the VMs on other healthy hosts in the cluster.
- C) DRS immediately rebalances the workload across the remaining hosts.
- D) vMotion automatically migrates the VMs to another host before the failure occurs.

Correct Answer: B) HA automatically restarts the VMs on other healthy hosts in the cluster.

Explanation:

In a vSphere HA cluster, if an ESXi host fails, HA automatically restarts the VMs that were running on the failed host onto other healthy hosts in the cluster. This ensures minimal downtime for the applications running in the virtual environment. DRS (Distributed Resource Scheduler) may rebalance resources after the VMs are restarted, but the primary role of HA is to ensure that VMs are restarted in case of host failure.

Exam Tip: Understand the roles of HA, DRS, and vMotion in ensuring high availability, load balancing, and zero-downtime migrations in vSphere environments.

➢ Approach to Exam Questions
➢ Read the Question Carefully:
➢ Ensure you understand the context of the question. Look for key terms such as vMotion, HA, or DRS to determine which vSphere feature is being referenced.

Eliminate Wrong Answers:

In multiple-choice questions, eliminate the obviously incorrect answers to narrow down your options. This can improve your chances of selecting the correct answer.

Scenario-Based Questions:

These questions often describe real-world problems. Focus on identifying the root cause and using logical troubleshooting steps to resolve the issue.

Familiarity with Command-Line Tools:

Some questions may require knowledge of command-line tools like ESXTOP, PowerCLI, or SSH commands for troubleshooting. Ensure you understand the basic commands used for managing and troubleshooting vSphere environments.

By practicing these types of questions, you'll gain the confidence needed to excel in the VMware vSphere 8.x Professional certification exam.

Detailed Answers and Explanations

This section provides detailed explanations for each of the questions in the previous subchapter. By understanding the rationale behind both the correct and incorrect answers, you will gain deeper insights into core vSphere concepts. Additionally, we'll highlight key points to remember for tackling similar questions on the VMware vSphere 8.x Professional certification exam.

Question 1: Virtualization Fundamentals

What is the primary benefit of virtualization in a vSphere environment?

Correct Answer: C) Consolidation of workloads to maximize hardware resource utilization

Explanation: Virtualization allows multiple virtual machines (VMs) to run on a single physical server, maximizing the usage of hardware resources like CPU, memory, and storage. By consolidating workloads, organizations can reduce the number of physical servers they need, leading to cost savings in hardware, energy, and space.

Incorrect Options:

A: Virtualization actually decreases hardware costs by reducing the need for physical servers.

B: While virtualization can enhance performance, it does not provide direct hardware access like bare-metal installations, which is why this option is incorrect.

D: Virtualization simplifies management through centralized tools, such as vCenter Server, so it doesn't increase complexity.

Key Point: Focus on the efficiency and cost benefits that virtualization provides when studying for similar questions on the exam.

Question 2: vSphere Architecture (Scenario-Based)

Scenario: A new ESXi host is added to the cluster, but it cannot connect to vCenter Server. What is the most likely cause of the connection issue, and how can you resolve it?

Correct Answer: C) The host's management network is down, and you need to restart the management agents.

Explanation: The vCenter Server communicates with ESXi hosts through the management network. If the management network is down, vCenter cannot establish a connection with the host. Restarting the host management agents (hostd and vpxa) often resolves the issue.

Command: You can restart the agents using services.sh restart through an SSH connection to the ESXi host.

Incorrect Options:

A: VLAN misconfiguration could cause network issues, but it's not the most likely cause here.

B: An incompatible ESXi version would lead to more explicit errors rather than a simple connectivity issue.

D: A full vCenter database could cause performance issues, but it wouldn't prevent a new host from being added.

Key Point: When troubleshooting ESXi connection issues, always check the management network and restart the management agents.

Question 3: Networking

What is the purpose of a vSphere Distributed Switch (vDS)?

Correct Answer: A) It provides centralized management for multiple ESXi hosts' networking configurations.

Explanation: A vSphere Distributed Switch (vDS) centralizes the management of networking across multiple ESXi hosts, allowing administrators to apply consistent networking policies and settings across the environment. It helps in managing network configurations, traffic shaping, and network security features across the entire vSphere cluster.

Incorrect Options:

B: VMs communicate through virtual and physical network interfaces via the ESXi host, not bypassing it.

C: vDS does not automate VLAN creation on physical switches.

D: While each VM has its own virtual network adapter, this is not a unique feature of a vDS but a characteristic of all vSphere networking.

Key Point: Understand the role of a vDS in managing and centralizing network configurations across hosts.

Question 4: Storage (Scenario-Based)

Scenario: A VM on an NFS datastore is showing degraded performance. What tool should you use first?

Correct Answer: C) Check the NFS datastore latency using vSphere Performance Charts.

Explanation: When storage performance is degraded, checking the latency on the datastore is a critical first step. vSphere Performance Charts provide detailed metrics, including I/O operations per second (IOPS), latency, and throughput. High datastore latency can indicate storage contention or an issue with the network connection to the NFS server.

Incorrect Options:

A: Migrating the VM with Storage vMotion might be a corrective action later, but first, you need to identify the cause of the performance degradation.

B: Increasing the NFS server's memory could help in certain cases, but you need to diagnose the issue first.

D: Adjusting the VM's memory allocation won't directly resolve storage-related issues.

Key Point: For storage-related performance issues, datastore latency is a key indicator to monitor using vSphere Performance Charts.

Question 5: High Availability (HA)

In a vSphere High Availability (HA) cluster, what happens when an ESXi host fails?

Correct Answer: B) HA automatically restarts the VMs on other healthy hosts in the cluster.

Explanation: vSphere HA is designed to ensure uptime by restarting VMs on other available hosts in the event of an ESXi host failure. This minimizes downtime and keeps critical applications running with minimal disruption. The primary function of HA is to recover VMs automatically when a host fails, rather than preventing failures or performing live migrations (which is the role of vMotion).

Incorrect Options:

A: HA does not permanently shut down VMs—it restarts them.

C: DRS may rebalance workloads post-failover, but it is not directly involved in the restart process.

D: vMotion performs live migrations but requires the host to be healthy; it does not migrate VMs after a host failure.

Key Point: vSphere HA focuses on restarting VMs on healthy hosts after a host failure, not on live migrations or preventing failures.

EXAM PREPARATION TIPS

➢ **Familiarize Yourself with Common Scenarios:** The vSphere exam often includes real-world troubleshooting and operational scenarios. Practicing these scenarios and understanding how to diagnose issues using VMware tools will help you excel in the exam.

➢ **Understand Key Features of vSphere Components:** Focus on understanding the purpose and functionality of key vSphere features, such as vMotion, HA, DRS, and Distributed Switches (vDS). Knowing when and how to use these features will be critical to answering both multiple-choice and scenario-based questions.

➢ **Use VMware Documentation and Hands-On Labs:** Access to VMware's official documentation and hands-on practice through VMware Hands-on Labs will provide deeper insights and help solidify your understanding of vSphere concepts.

➢ **Focus on Monitoring Tools:** Be comfortable with using vSphere Performance Charts, ESXTOP, and other monitoring tools to diagnose performance issues in storage, networking, and host configurations.

By understanding the rationale behind both correct and incorrect answers, you will be better equipped to handle similar questions on the exam.

Practice Exam Simulation

This section simulates a practice exam for the VMware vSphere 8.x Professional certification. The questions below are designed to mimic the format of the actual exam, including both multiple-choice and scenario-based questions. At the end of the section, detailed answers and explanations are provided to help assess your understanding of core vSphere concepts and preparedness for the certification exam.

Multiple-Choice Questions

Question 1: Virtualization Basics

Which component is responsible for managing multiple virtual machines on a single ESXi host?

A) vCenter Server

B) vSphere Client

C) ESXi Hypervisor

D) Distributed Resource Scheduler (DRS)

Question 2: vMotion and Storage vMotion

What is the primary difference between vMotion and Storage vMotion?

A) vMotion migrates a VM between hosts; Storage vMotion migrates VM files between datastores.

B) vMotion migrates a VM between datastores; Storage vMotion migrates VMs between networks.

C) vMotion requires downtime, whereas Storage vMotion is live.

D) vMotion is used for failover; Storage vMotion is used for backup.

\

Question 3: High Availability (HA)

What is the purpose of Admission Control in a vSphere HA cluster?

A) To manage VM migration between clusters

B) To ensure that there are enough resources to restart VMs after a host failure

C) To enforce backup policies for high availability

D) To prevent unauthorized access to VMs

Question 4: vSphere Distributed Resource Scheduler (DRS)

Which DRS automation level allows vCenter to recommend, but not automatically perform, VM migrations?

A) Manual

B) Semi-Automated

C) Fully Automated

D) Disabled

Question 5: vSphere Networking

What is the role of Network I/O Control (NIOC) in a vSphere Distributed Switch (vDS)?

A) To enable storage replication over network traffic

B) To limit the amount of network traffic used by specific VMs or traffic types

C) To enforce security policies across multiple VLANs

D) To increase the bandwidth available to physical NICs

Question 6: vSAN

Which feature of vSAN enables the use of local storage devices across multiple hosts to form a single distributed datastore?

A) vMotion

B) vSAN Network

C) vSAN Storage Pool

D) Datastore Cluster

Question 7: vSphere Security

Which of the following security features provides encryption for virtual machine disks in vSphere?

A) vSphere Native Key Provider

B) vSphere HA

C) vSphere Lockdown Mode

D) vSphere TPM (Trusted Platform Module)

Scenario-Based Questions

Scenario 1: Performance Troubleshooting

Scenario: You are managing a vSphere environment where a VM is experiencing high CPU ready times, indicating that it is waiting for CPU resources. Other VMs on the same host are not experiencing similar issues.

Question: What could be the most likely cause, and how would you resolve it?

A) The VM has too many vCPUs assigned and should be resized.

B) The physical CPU on the host is failing.

C) The VM is experiencing memory ballooning.

D) The VM's disk I/O is creating contention.

Scenario 2: Storage Capacity

Scenario: You receive a warning that a datastore is running low on capacity. After investigating, you discover that snapshots on several VMs have grown large and are consuming significant space.

Question: What should you do to reclaim the storage space?

A) Perform a Storage vMotion to another datastore.

B) Consolidate the snapshots to commit the changes and free up space.

C) Increase the capacity of the datastore by adding additional storage.

D) Shut down the VMs and remove the snapshots.

Scenario 3: VM Migration

Scenario: You need to migrate a virtual machine that is running a mission-critical application to another host for maintenance. The application cannot tolerate downtime.

Question: Which feature should you use to perform the migration without service interruption?

A) Cold Migration

B) vMotion

C) Storage vMotion

D) Fault Tolerance

PRACTICE EXAM ANSWERS AND EXPLANATIONS

Question 1: Virtualization Basics

Correct Answer: C) ESXi Hypervisor

Explanation: The ESXi hypervisor is responsible for managing multiple virtual machines on a single host. It allocates resources like CPU, memory, and storage to VMs and isolates them from one another. vCenter Server centrally manages multiple hosts, but the hypervisor manages VMs at the host level.

Question 2: vMotion and Storage vMotion

Correct Answer: A) vMotion migrates a VM between hosts; Storage vMotion migrates VM files between datastores.

Explanation: vMotion allows a VM to move between hosts with no downtime, while Storage vMotion migrates the VM's storage files between datastores without service interruption. Both processes are live migrations.

Question 3: High Availability (HA)

Correct Answer: B) To ensure that there are enough resources to restart VMs after a host failure

Explanation: Admission Control in a vSphere HA cluster ensures that sufficient resources are reserved to restart all virtual machines if a host fails. This prevents oversubscription of resources and guarantees that VMs can be restarted on the remaining hosts.

Question 4: vSphere Distributed Resource Scheduler (DRS)

Correct Answer: B) Semi-Automated

Explanation: Semi-Automated DRS makes recommendations for VM migrations but requires administrator approval to complete them. In contrast, Fully Automated performs migrations automatically, and Manual requires the administrator to both recommend and approve migrations.

Question 5: vSphere Networking

Correct Answer: B) To limit the amount of network traffic used by specific VMs or traffic types

Explanation: Network I/O Control (NIOC) manages and limits network traffic on a vSphere Distributed Switch (vDS) by allocating bandwidth to different traffic types, such as VM traffic, vMotion, and storage replication.

Question 6: vSAN

Correct Answer: C) vSAN Storage Pool

Explanation: vSAN aggregates local storage devices (SSD or HDD) from multiple hosts to create a single distributed datastore. This datastore is then used by VMs, enabling hyperconverged storage across the cluster.

Question 7: vSphere Security

Correct Answer: A) vSphere Native Key Provider

Explanation: vSphere Native Key Provider is a built-in key management solution that allows for the encryption of VM disks (data at rest). This ensures that VM data is protected, even if a virtual disk file is copied or stolen.

Scenario 1: Performance Troubleshooting

Correct Answer: A) The VM has too many vCPUs assigned and should be resized.

Explanation: High CPU ready time usually indicates that a VM is waiting for CPU resources because it has been over-provisioned with vCPUs. Reducing the number of vCPUs can improve performance by reducing contention with other VMs on the same host.

Scenario 2: Storage Capacity

Correct Answer: B) Consolidate the snapshots to commit the changes and free up space.

Explanation: Snapshots consume additional space as they grow over time. Consolidating snapshots merges the changes into the base disk, freeing up space on the datastore.

Scenario 3: VM Migration

Correct Answer: B) vMotion

Explanation: vMotion allows you to migrate a running VM between hosts with no downtime. This is the ideal solution for migrating a VM running a mission-critical application that cannot tolerate service interruptions.

Final Thoughts And Exam Preparation Tips

➤ **Understand Core Concepts:** Master the basics of vMotion, HA, DRS, vSAN, and NIOC as they are common topics on the exam.

➤ **Practice with Real-World Scenarios:** Scenario-based questions often mirror real-world operational problems. Use VMware labs to practice troubleshooting and configuration tasks.

➤ **Study Key Features:** Focus on vSphere features like vMotion, Snapshots, and vSphere HA, as these are integral to managing VMware environments efficiently.

➤ **Time Management:** On the exam, quickly eliminate obviously incorrect answers to narrow down your choices and focus on the correct option.

By practicing with this simulated exam, you will strengthen your knowledge of VMware vSphere and gain the confidence to handle similar questions on the actual certification test.

SAMPLE QUESTIONS ON CORE VSPHERE CONCEPTS (2)

Virtualization Fundamentals

Question 1: What is the primary advantage of server virtualization?

A) It increases physical hardware requirements

B) It allows multiple operating systems to run on a single physical machine

C) It limits the number of virtual machines (VMs) that can be created

D) It creates security vulnerabilities across virtual machines

Answer: B) It allows multiple operating systems to run on a single physical machine

Explanation: Virtualization enables multiple operating systems to run on one physical machine using a hypervisor. This improves hardware efficiency and reduces costs. Options A, C, and D are incorrect because virtualization reduces hardware requirements and enhances, rather than limits, security when configured properly.

Question 2: Which of the following is a Type 1 hypervisor?

A) VMware Workstation

B) VMware Fusion

C) VMware ESXi

D) Oracle VirtualBox

Answer: C) VMware ESXi

Explanation: Type 1 hypervisors (bare-metal) like VMware ESXi run directly on hardware, while Type 2 hypervisors (e.g., VMware Workstation) run on top of an operating system. Options A, B, and D refer to Type 2 hypervisors.

Question 3: What is the role of vCenter Server in a vSphere environment?

A) It directly manages all hardware resources

B) It centralizes management of multiple ESXi hosts

C) It manages operating systems inside virtual machines

D) It serves as a hypervisor for VMs

Answer: B) It centralizes management of multiple ESXi hosts

Explanation: vCenter Server is used to centrally manage multiple ESXi hosts and the resources they provide. It does not manage individual hardware directly (A) or serve as a hypervisor itself (D).

vSphere Architecture

Question 4: Which vSphere component is responsible for running virtual machines?

A) vCenter Server

B) vSphere Client

C) VMware ESXi

D) vSAN

Answer: C) VMware ESXi

Explanation: The ESXi hypervisor is responsible for running virtual machines by abstracting hardware resources. vCenter Server manages multiple hosts, but ESXi is the core hypervisor running on each physical server.

Question 5: What does a vCenter Server Appliance (VCSA) use to store data?

A) vSAN

B) External storage arrays

C) A built-in PostgreSQL database

D) Virtual machine snapshots

Answer: C) A built-in PostgreSQL database

Explanation: The vCenter Server Appliance (VCSA) uses an embedded PostgreSQL database to store inventory and configuration data, making it a self-contained management platform. External storage is not used to store the VCSA's own data.

Question 6: Which feature of vSphere allows for dynamic allocation of resources to virtual machines?

A) vSphere HA

B) vSphere DRS

C) vSAN

D) FT (Fault Tolerance)

Answer: B) vSphere DRS

Explanation: Distributed Resource Scheduler (DRS) dynamically balances resources (CPU, memory) across ESXi hosts in a cluster based on VM workloads.

Networking

Question 7: What is the purpose of a vSphere Distributed Switch (vDS)?

A) To provide basic networking for a single ESXi host

B) To centralize and manage networking across multiple ESXi hosts

C) To replicate storage traffic between hosts

D) To allow communication between vCenter Server and virtual machines

Answer: B) To centralize and manage networking across multiple ESXi hosts

Explanation: vDS allows centralized management of networking across multiple hosts, providing consistent policies for networking features such as VLANs and port groups.

Question 8: Which of the following is a benefit of using VLANs in vSphere networking?

A) It reduces the need for physical NICs

B) It secures VMs by segmenting traffic within a single virtual switch

C) It simplifies the vSphere upgrade process

D) It increases the physical footprint of the environment

Answer: B) It secures VMs by segmenting traffic within a single virtual switch

Explanation: VLANs are used to logically segment network traffic, improving security and isolation between different virtual machines and traffic types.

Question 9: How does Network I/O Control (NIOC) help in vSphere Distributed Switch?

A) It prevents network failures by duplicating traffic

B) It allocates and prioritizes bandwidth based on traffic type

C) It improves storage performance

D) It centralizes ESXi storage management

Answer: B) It allocates and prioritizes bandwidth based on traffic type

Explanation: NIOC manages and allocates network bandwidth dynamically, ensuring that critical traffic types (e.g., vMotion, storage) receive sufficient bandwidth during congestion.

Storage

Question 10: Which type of storage can be used for both block-based and file-based data?

A) NFS

B) iSCSI

C) Fibre Channel

D) vSAN

Answer: D) Vsan

Explanation: vSAN aggregates local storage across hosts and can handle both block and file-based data storage. NFS is file-based, and iSCSI and Fibre Channel are block-based.

Question 11: What is the role of a datastore in vSphere?

A) It provides a backup mechanism for VMs

B) It hosts virtual machine files and disks

C) It stores network configuration data

D) It replicates VMs between ESXi hosts

Answer: B) It hosts virtual machine files and disks

Explanation: A datastore is a storage location used to store virtual machine files, such as virtual disks, configuration files, and snapshots.

Question 12: What is Storage I/O Control (SIOC) used for in a vSphere environment?

A) To manage backup schedules for virtual machines

B) To allocate and prioritize storage resources to virtual machines

C) To enhance security by limiting data access

D) To automate the creation of snapshots

Answer: B) To allocate and prioritize storage resources to virtual machines

Explanation: Storage I/O Control (SIOC) dynamically allocates storage resources to VMs based on demand, preventing any one VM from monopolizing storage resources.

Security

Question 13: Which feature of vSphere can prevent unauthorized access to an ESXi host?

A) Role-Based Access Control (RBAC)

B) Lockdown Mode

C) Distributed Resource Scheduler (DRS)

D) vMotion

Answer: B) Lockdown Mode

Explanation: Lockdown Mode restricts direct access to an ESXi host, ensuring that all administrative access is controlled through vCenter Server.

Question 14: What is Role-Based Access Control (RBAC) in vSphere?

A) A method to allocate network bandwidth

B) A system to assign permissions to users based on their role

C) A mechanism to replicate VMs between datastores

D) A feature that prevents VM migration

Answer: B) A system to assign permissions to users based on their role

Explanation: RBAC assigns different access levels and permissions based on the user's role in the organization, improving security and management.

Question 15: Which of the following provides encryption for virtual machines in vSphere?

A) vSphere Native Key Provider

B) vMotion

C) NFS

D) Storage I/O Control (SIOC)

Answer: A) vSphere Native Key Provider

Explanation: The vSphere Native Key Provider allows encryption of VM disks and other sensitive data at rest.

Virtualization Fundamentals (Continued)

Question 16: Which feature enables the use of shared storage to store VMs, allowing for better flexibility and availability in a virtualized environment?

A) DRS

B) vSAN

C) HA

D) vMotion

Answer: B) vSAN

Explanation: vSAN aggregates local storage from multiple hosts into a shared datastore, allowing for high availability and flexibility for storing virtual machine data. DRS handles resource allocation, HA restarts VMs after a host failure, and vMotion is used to migrate running VMs between hosts without downtime.

Question 17: What does the "Virtual Machine File System (VMFS)" provide in vSphere environments?

A) A file system for configuring VLANs

B) A file system to store VMs and snapshots across multiple ESXi hosts

C) A distributed network file system for external storage

D) An encrypted storage area for virtual machine backups

Answer: B) A file system to store VMs and snapshots across multiple ESXi hosts

Explanation: VMFS is a clustered file system used by ESXi hosts to store virtual machine files and snapshots. It supports concurrent access to the same virtual machines across multiple ESXi hosts, allowing for features like vMotion and HA.

Question 18: Which of the following is true regarding Type 2 hypervisors?

A) They run directly on top of physical hardware

B) They require a host operating system

C) They offer better performance than Type 1 hypervisors

D) VMware ESXi is an example of a Type 2 hypervisor

Answer: B) They require a host operating system

Explanation: Type 2 hypervisors run on top of an existing operating system (e.g., VMware Workstation). In contrast, Type 1 hypervisors like ESXi run directly on the physical hardware without a host OS, providing better performance.

Question 19: Which of the following features can provide fault tolerance for VMs by creating an exact replica on a separate ESXi host?

A) vMotion

B) DRS

C) HA

D) FT (Fault Tolerance)

Answer: D) FT (Fault Tolerance)

Explanation: VMware Fault Tolerance (FT) creates a live, secondary instance of a virtual machine on a separate host, ensuring no downtime if the primary instance fails. vMotion and DRS are related to resource management and VM migration, while HA restarts VMs after a failure, but not without a brief downtime.

vSphere Architecture (Continued)

Question 20: In vSphere, what is the purpose of vCenter Enhanced Linked Mode?

A) It links ESXi hosts to shared datastores

B) It provides redundancy for vCenter Server

C) It allows management of multiple vCenter Servers from a single interface

D) It links virtual machines for load balancing

Answer: C) It allows management of multiple vCenter Servers from a single interface

Explanation: Enhanced Linked Mode in vSphere allows administrators to manage multiple vCenter Servers from a single interface, enabling centralized control of larger environments without logging into each vCenter Server instance individually.

Question 21: Which of the following components can be managed directly using the vSphere Client?

A) ESXi Hosts

B) vSAN Storage Policies

C) VM Hardware Settings

D) All of the above

Answer: D) All of the above

Explanation: The vSphere Client is the main interface for managing various components of the vSphere environment, including ESXi hosts, vSAN storage, and virtual machine hardware settings.

Question 22: What is the main purpose of the vSphere Distributed Resource Scheduler (DRS) in a cluster?

A) To balance network traffic across physical NICs

B) To automatically distribute workloads across ESXi hosts based on resource utilization

C) To perform automatic backups of virtual machines

D) To monitor security configurations across ESXi hosts

Answer: B) To automatically distribute workloads across ESXi hosts based on resource utilization

Explanation: DRS automatically balances workloads across ESXi hosts based on real-time resource utilization (e.g., CPU, memory), ensuring efficient resource allocation and minimizing performance bottlenecks.

Networking (Continued)

Question 23: Which of the following is required to enable vSphere vMotion for a virtual machine?

A) The source and destination hosts must have shared storage

B) Both hosts must have the same version of ESXi

C) The virtual machine must be powered off during the migration

D) The virtual machine must have a dedicated network card

Answer: A) The source and destination hosts must have shared storage

Explanation: To perform a vMotion, both the source and destination ESXi hosts need access to the same shared storage to ensure continuity during the migration. Options B and C are not requirements for vMotion, as different ESXi versions are supported, and the VM remains powered on.

Question 24: What is a vSphere Standard Switch (vSS) used for?

A) To manage virtual machine network traffic on a single ESXi host

B) To manage networking across multiple hosts in a cluster

C) To manage external network traffic only

D) To connect physical switches with virtual machine storage

Answer: A) To manage virtual machine network traffic on a single ESXi host

Explanation: A vSphere Standard Switch (vSS) is used for managing network traffic between virtual machines on a single ESXi host. It is limited to local host traffic, unlike a vSphere Distributed Switch (vDS), which works across multiple hosts.

Question 25: What is Port Mirroring in a vSphere Distributed Switch (vDS)?

A) A method of duplicating traffic for monitoring and analysis

B) A way to extend virtual machine storage

C) A feature to duplicate CPU allocation for critical VMs

D) A method of migrating VMs without downtime

Answer: A) A method of duplicating traffic for monitoring and analysis

Explanation: Port Mirroring allows administrators to duplicate network traffic from a port or group of ports on a distributed switch to another location, typically for monitoring or troubleshooting network performance and security.

Storage (Continued)

Question 26: Which of the following is a file-based storage protocol commonly used in vSphere environments?

A) Fibre Channel

B) Iscsi

C) NFS

D) Vsan

Answer: C) NFS

Explanation: Network File System (NFS) is a file-based protocol used in vSphere to access storage over a network. Fibre Channel and iSCSI are block-based protocols, while vSAN aggregates local storage across hosts into a shared datastore.

Question 27: What is the purpose of vSAN Fault Domains?

A) To isolate network traffic

B) To provide enhanced security for VM data

C) To protect against site-level failures by placing data across different racks

D) To limit CPU usage for resource-intensive VMs

Answer: C) To protect against site-level failures by placing data across different racks

Explanation: vSAN Fault Domains allow you to group hosts in different physical locations, such as separate racks, to protect against rack-level or site-level failures by ensuring data is spread across those locations.

Question 28: What happens when Storage I/O Control (SIOC) detects high latency on a datastore?

A) It automatically shuts down low-priority VMs

B) It dynamically allocates I/O resources to prioritize critical VMs

C) It migrates VMs to a new datastore

D) It increases the memory allocation for affected VMs

Answer: B) It dynamically allocates I/O resources to prioritize critical VMs

Explanation: SIOC monitors latency on shared datastores and dynamically adjusts I/O allocation to prioritize critical VMs when high latency is detected.

Security (Continued)

Question 29: Which of the following features restricts local and remote access to an ESXi host?

A) Lockdown Mode

B) vSAN

C) Role-Based Access Control (RBAC)

D) vMotion

Answer: A) Lockdown Mode

Explanation: Lockdown Mode restricts direct access to an ESXi host, requiring all management to be conducted through vCenter Server to increase security.

Question 30: What is the main function of vSphere Encryption?

A) To encrypt VM disks and files for security

B) To protect the ESXi management network

C) To encrypt vSphere Client connections

D) To encrypt network traffic between VMs

Answer: A) To encrypt VM disks and files for security

Explanation: vSphere Encryption is used to encrypt VM disks (VMDKs) and files to ensure that data at rest is protected from unauthorized access.

Automation

Question 31: Which PowerCLI command is used to create a new virtual machine in vSphere?

A) New-VM

B) Create-VM

C) Start-VM

D) Deploy-VM

Answer: A) New-VM

Explanation: New-VM is the PowerCLI cmdlet used to create a new virtual machine. The command allows you to specify properties such as the VM name, resource pool, datastore, number of CPUs, and memory size. Options B, C, and D are incorrect because they are not valid PowerCLI commands for VM creation.

Question 32: In vSphere, which scripting tool can be used for automating and managing tasks such as virtual machine provisioning and storage configuration?

A) vSphere API

B) PowerCLI

C) ESXTOP

D) vCenter Server

Answer: B) PowerCLI

Explanation: PowerCLI is a powerful scripting tool based on PowerShell, designed to automate vSphere management tasks like VM provisioning, configuration, and resource management. vSphere API is another automation tool but more developer-oriented, while ESXTOP is for performance monitoring.

Question 33: What is a key use of the vSphere API?

A) To manually create backup jobs

B) To automate and integrate vSphere features into third-party tools

C) To monitor ESXi host power consumption

D) To limit user access to specific VMs

Answer: B) To automate and integrate vSphere features into third-party tools

Explanation: The vSphere API allows developers to create custom scripts or integrate vSphere functionality into third-party tools for automation and extended management capabilities. It provides programmatic access to vSphere features.

Question 34: Which of the following PowerCLI cmdlets is used to retrieve a list of all virtual machines in a vCenter Server?

A) Get-VM

B) List-VM

C) Show-VMs

D) Query-VM

Answer: A) Get-VM

Explanation: Get-VM retrieves a list of all virtual machines within the vCenter Server or ESXi host. This command is frequently used to gather VM information or modify virtual machine settings.

Question 35: Which vSphere API is more modern and lightweight, offering RESTful access to vSphere features?

A) SOAP-based Web Services API

B) vSphere Automation SDK

C) VMware Workstation API

D) VMware SDK

Answer: B) vSphere Automation SDK

Explanation: The vSphere Automation SDK offers RESTful access to VMware's vSphere features, making it a modern and lightweight option for developers to interact with vSphere. It is easier to integrate with cloud-native and modern application workflows compared to the SOAP-based API.

Scenario-Based Questions

Scenario 4: ESXi Host Troubleshooting

Scenario: A host in your vSphere cluster has unexpectedly gone into maintenance mode, and you need to bring it back online. However, it remains stuck in maintenance mode even after attempting to exit.

Question: What action should you take first to troubleshoot this issue?

A) Restart the vCenter Server

B) Reboot the host using the vSphere Client

C) Check for ongoing maintenance tasks like vMotion or Storage vMotion

D) Remove the host from the cluster and re-add it

Answer: C) Check for ongoing maintenance tasks like vMotion or Storage vMotion

Explanation: If a host is stuck in maintenance mode, the first step should be to check whether there are ongoing tasks like vMotion or Storage vMotion preventing it from exiting maintenance mode. Rebooting or removing the host should be considered only if no active tasks are found.

Scenario 5: Virtual Machine Disk Issues

Scenario: A virtual machine on an NFS datastore has started exhibiting poor disk performance. Other VMs using the same datastore seem to be operating normally.

Question: What is the first step in troubleshooting the VM's poor performance?

A) Increase the VM's memory allocation

B) Check the NFS datastore's I/O latency using vSphere Performance Charts

C) Migrate the VM to a new datastore

D) Check the VM's CPU and memory allocation

Answer: B) Check the NFS datastore's I/O latency using vSphere Performance Charts

Explanation: Since the issue is disk-related, checking the datastore's I/O latency using vSphere Performance Charts will help determine whether the storage backend is the source of the performance degradation. Increasing memory or migrating the VM may not resolve the issue if it's storage-related.

Scenario 6: VM Snapshot Management

Scenario: You discover that several VMs in your vSphere environment have snapshots that are weeks old, consuming significant datastore space. What is the recommended approach to address this issue?

A) Delete the VM snapshots immediately

B) Consolidate the snapshots

C) Shut down the VM and then delete the snapshots

D) Migrate the VMs to another datastore to free space

Answer: B) Consolidate the snapshots

Explanation: Snapshot consolidation ensures that changes saved in the snapshots are committed to the base disk, freeing up datastore space. Deleting snapshots without consolidating them could cause data loss, and migrating VMs won't directly address the issue of snapshot growth.

Storage

Question 36: What is the function of a Storage Policy-Based Management (SPBM) in vSphere?

A) It automatically backs up virtual machines to the cloud

B) It defines rules for provisioning and managing storage for VMs based on policy-driven automation

C) It encrypts datastore-level storage for security

D) It controls network traffic between datastores

Answer: B) It defines rules for provisioning and managing storage for VMs based on policy-driven automation

Explanation: SPBM allows for policy-driven storage management, enabling administrators to set rules for provisioning storage and managing storage resources for virtual machines, ensuring consistent performance and availability.

Question 37: Which storage protocol in vSphere allows block-level access over TCP/IP?

A) NFS

B) iSCSI

C) Fibre Channel

D) VMFS

Answer: B) iSCSI

Explanation: iSCSI allows block-level storage access over a TCP/IP network, making it a popular choice for vSphere environments where traditional Fibre Channel SAN is unavailable.

Question 38: Which of the following statements is true about VMFS?

A) It is used to create a datastore for NFS storage

B) It provides a clustered file system across ESXi hosts

C) It supports only local storage

D) It automatically backs up VMs in a cluster

Answer: B) It provides a clustered file system across ESXi hosts

Explanation: VMFS (Virtual Machine File System) is a clustered file system used in vSphere environments to allow multiple ESXi hosts to access the same datastore concurrently, enabling features like vMotion and HA.

Question 39: Which of the following is a block-based storage protocol in vSphere?

A) NFS

B) iSCSI

C) SMB

D) FTP

Answer: B) iSCSI

Explanation: iSCSI is a block-based storage protocol that allows ESXi hosts to access remote storage devices over an IP network. NFS and SMB are file-based protocols.

Question 40: What happens when a datastore is set to thin provisioning?

A) All disk space is allocated immediately

B) Disk space is allocated dynamically as data is written to the VM

C) VMs will have limited access to datastore resources

D) It ensures that the VM's performance is maximized

Answer: B) Disk space is allocated dynamically as data is written to the VM

Explanation: With thin provisioning, storage is allocated to VMs dynamically as needed, rather than reserving the entire disk space upfront. This allows for more efficient use of datastore capacity.

Security (Continued)

Question 41: What is vSphere Lockdown Mode designed to do?

A) It prevents the creation of virtual machines

B) It restricts direct access to ESXi hosts from the vSphere Client

C) It disables the use of virtual switches

D) It encrypts all communication between ESXi hosts

Answer: B) It restricts direct access to ESXi hosts from the vSphere Client

Explanation: Lockdown Mode restricts direct access to ESXi hosts by requiring that all management be conducted through vCenter Server, improving security and reducing potential attack vectors. This enhances the security posture of the environment by preventing unauthorized access to ESXi hosts.

Question 42: Which feature allows for role-based access control (RBAC) in vSphere?

A) Network I/O Control

B) vCenter Single Sign-On (SSO)

C) vSAN Fault Domains

D) Distributed Resource Scheduler (DRS)

Answer: B) vCenter Single Sign-On (SSO)

Explanation: vCenter Single Sign-On (SSO) facilitates role-based access control (RBAC) by allowing administrators to manage user access and assign roles and permissions to different users, based on their tasks within the vSphere environment.

Question 43: What is the primary use case for vSphere Native Key Provider (NKP)?

A) Managing network bandwidth for VMs

B) Encrypting virtual machine disk files (VMDKs)

C) Monitoring the health of ESXi hosts

D) Automating VM provisioning across multiple hosts

Answer: B) Encrypting virtual machine disk files (VMDKs)

Explanation: vSphere Native Key Provider (NKP) is used for managing encryption keys, allowing for encryption of VM disk files (VMDKs) to ensure data at rest is secure. NKP does not manage network bandwidth or health monitoring.

Question 44: Which of the following describes vSphere Certificate Management?

A) A mechanism to store network traffic data

B) A feature to manage SSL certificates used to secure communication between vSphere components

C) A method for encrypting VM data between hosts

D) A tool for limiting CPU usage for specific workloads

Answer: B) A feature to manage SSL certificates used to secure communication between vSphere components

Explanation: vSphere Certificate Management handles SSL certificates to secure communication between various vSphere components, such as vCenter Server, ESXi hosts, and vSphere Clients, ensuring encrypted and secure data transmission within the infrastructure.

Question 45: Which encryption feature does vSphere 8.x support natively without needing external key management servers (KMS)?

A) Transparent Data Encryption (TDE)

B) Encrypted vMotion

C) VM Snapshot Encryption

D) Virtual SAN Encryption

Answer: B) Encrypted vMotion

Explanation: Encrypted vMotion is a feature that allows the migration of virtual machines between hosts while encrypting the data in transit, without needing an external Key Management Server (KMS).

Automation (Continued)

Question 46: Which PowerCLI cmdlet is used to power on a virtual machine?

A) New-VM

B) Start-VM

C) Enable-VM

D) Invoke-VM

Answer: B) Start-VM

Explanation: Start-VM is the PowerCLI cmdlet used to power on virtual machines. It is part of the automation tools used to manage VMs programmatically.

Question 47: What does the Get-VMHost cmdlet in PowerCLI retrieve?

A) The current state of virtual machines

B) A list of all hosts connected to vCenter

C) The number of CPU cores on a virtual machine

D) The memory usage of virtual machines

Answer: B) A list of all hosts connected to vCenter

Explanation: The Get-VMHost cmdlet retrieves information about ESXi hosts connected to the vCenter Server. It provides details about each host's status, resources, and configuration.

Question 48: Which of the following is a common use case for vSphere PowerCLI?

A) Automating network device configuration outside of VMware

B) Managing ESXi host BIOS settings

C) Automating the provisioning of virtual machines

D) Replacing vCenter Server with a command-line interface

Answer: C) Automating the provisioning of virtual machines

Explanation: vSphere PowerCLI is used primarily to automate various vSphere tasks, including the provisioning of virtual machines, managing clusters, configuring storage, and other tasks that would otherwise require manual intervention through the vSphere Client.

Question 49: What is a benefit of using vSphere API over PowerCLI?

A) Easier to use for basic VM management

B) Higher level of integration with third-party tools and advanced automation

C) Pre-built scripts for managing network settings

D) It provides an alternative to using vCenter for VM provisioning

Answer: B) Higher level of integration with third-party tools and advanced automation

Explanation: The vSphere API allows developers to build advanced integrations with third-party tools and automate complex tasks. PowerCLI is simpler for basic administrative tasks but lacks the flexibility of deep integration available with the vSphere API.

Question 50: Which scripting language forms the basis of PowerCLI?

A) Bash

B) Python

C) PowerShell

D) JavaScript

Answer: C) PowerShell

Explanation: PowerCLI is built on Microsoft PowerShell, enabling administrators to script and automate vSphere-related tasks easily.

Virtualization Fundamentals (Continued)

Question 51: What is the main advantage of using virtual CPU (vCPU) over physical CPU in a virtualized environment?

A) It eliminates the need for physical processors

B) It allows overcommitting CPU resources for better efficiency

C) It automatically scales CPU resources with workload demands

D) It improves the security of virtual machines

Answer: B) It allows overcommitting CPU resources for better efficiency

Explanation: vCPUs allow overcommitting, meaning more virtual CPUs can be assigned to virtual machines than the available physical CPU cores. This improves efficiency by dynamically sharing the available CPU resources among VMs. Option A is incorrect because physical processors are still needed, and C does not automatically happen without configuration.

Question 52: What feature in vSphere ensures minimal downtime by keeping a secondary VM in sync with a primary VM, so that it can immediately take over in case of failure?

A) vSphere Replication

B) vSphere Fault Tolerance (FT)

C) vSphere DRS

D) vSAN

Answer: B) vSphere Fault Tolerance (FT)

Explanation: vSphere Fault Tolerance (FT) creates a secondary instance of a VM that is kept in sync with the primary VM. If the primary VM fails, the secondary VM takes over without downtime. vSphere Replication ensures data replication but does not handle real-time failover.

Question 53: What is the role of VMware Tools in a virtualized environment?

A) To manage and update physical hardware

B) To optimize virtual machine performance and provide guest OS functionality

C) To increase vSphere host capacity

D) To configure vSphere HA settings

Answer: B) To optimize virtual machine performance and provide guest OS functionality

Explanation: VMware Tools is a suite installed on guest operating systems that enhances VM performance, improves management, and enables features like mouse syncing, network improvements, and proper shutdown handling.

vSphere Architecture (Continued)

Question 54: What is the primary function of the vSphere HA Admission Control feature?

A) It limits the number of virtual machines that can be powered on

B) It ensures enough resources are reserved to restart VMs in case of a host failure

C) It replicates VMs between different hosts

D) It prevents unauthorized access to virtual machines

Answer: B) It ensures enough resources are reserved to restart VMs in case of a host failure

Explanation: Admission Control ensures that enough resources are always available to restart virtual machines on surviving hosts in case of an ESXi host failure, thereby maintaining high availability. It does not limit the number of powered-on VMs unless resource constraints would prevent failover.

Question 55: What is the benefit of enabling vSphere Enhanced vMotion Compatibility (EVC) in a cluster?

A) It improves VM networking performance

B) It standardizes the CPU features across hosts, enabling seamless VM migrations

C) It increases the physical memory on ESXi hosts

D) It allows distributed switches to support more VMs

Answer: B) It standardizes the CPU features across hosts, enabling seamless VM migrations

Explanation: Enhanced vMotion Compatibility (EVC) standardizes the CPU feature sets across all hosts in a cluster, ensuring that virtual machines can migrate between hosts even if they have different CPU architectures.

Networking (Continued)

Question 56: In a vSphere Distributed Switch (vDS), what does the Load-Based Teaming (LBT) feature do?

A) It distributes VM traffic based on the available CPU resources

B) It allocates bandwidth to VMs based on their I/O requirements

C) It dynamically balances network traffic based on the load across physical NICs

D) It mirrors network traffic for backup purposes

Answer: C) It dynamically balances network traffic based on the load across physical NICs

Explanation: Load-Based Teaming (LBT) dynamically adjusts the traffic distribution across physical NICs based on actual network load, ensuring efficient use of available bandwidth and improving performance.

Question 57: What does the Network I/O Control (NIOC) feature provide?

A) It increases memory allocation for critical virtual machines

B) It allows network bandwidth to be allocated based on traffic type

C) It creates a separate network for vSphere Replication

D) It performs live migrations of virtual machines across hosts

Answer: B) It allows network bandwidth to be allocated based on traffic type

Explanation: Network I/O Control (NIOC) allocates and prioritizes bandwidth for various types of network traffic (e.g., VM, management, storage), ensuring that critical traffic gets enough bandwidth during network congestion.

Question 58: Which of the following virtual networking options allows VMs on a vSphere Standard Switch (vSS) to communicate with each other and external networks?

A) Virtual NIC (vNIC)

B) Port Group

C) Distributed Switch

D) VMkernel Port

Answer: B) Port Group

Explanation: A Port Group on a vSphere Standard Switch allows virtual machines to communicate with each other and external networks. Port groups define network settings like VLANs and security policies for the VMs connected to the switch.

Storage (Continued)

Question 59: What does vSphere Storage DRS help achieve?

A) It dynamically allocates CPU and memory resources across VMs

B) It automatically places and balances virtual machine storage across datastores

C) It backs up all virtual machines to a remote datastore

D) It migrates virtual machines between hosts with no downtime

Answer: B) It automatically places and balances virtual machine storage across datastores

Explanation: vSphere Storage DRS provides automated placement of virtual machine storage on the most appropriate datastore based on capacity and performance metrics, helping to avoid storage bottlenecks.

Question 60: Which of the following storage technologies in vSphere allows the creation of a shared datastore across multiple ESXi hosts using local storage?

A) Fibre Channel

B) NFS

C) vSAN

D) iSCSI

Answer: C) vSAN

Explanation: vSAN aggregates local storage from ESXi hosts into a shared datastore that can be accessed by multiple hosts, enabling features like HA, DRS, and vMotion.

Question 61: Which of the following storage protocols is file-based?

A) NFS

B) Fibre Channel

C) iSCSI

D) VMFS

Answer: A) NFS

Explanation: Network File System (NFS) is a file-based storage protocol that allows ESXi hosts to access shared storage over a network. Fibre Channel and iSCSI are block-based storage protocols.

Question 62: What does thin provisioning of a virtual disk in vSphere do?

A) It allocates the entire disk space upfront

B) It allocates disk space only as data is written

C) It reduces the performance of VMs

D) It compresses the virtual disk to save space

Answer: B) It allocates disk space only as data is written

Explanation: Thin provisioning allows a virtual disk to consume space only as data is written to it, rather than reserving the entire disk space upfront. This optimizes storage utilization.

Security (Continued)

Question 63: What is the purpose of vSphere Trust Authority?

A) To manage user access to VMs

B) To secure and ensure the integrity of the infrastructure through hardware-backed security

C) To monitor virtual machine resource usage

D) To restrict access to distributed switches

Answer: B) To secure and ensure the integrity of the infrastructure through hardware-backed security

Explanation: vSphere Trust Authority (vTA) enhances security by creating a trusted infrastructure based on hardware-backed modules, such as Trusted Platform Module (TPM), ensuring the integrity of the ESXi hosts and the vCenter Server.

Question 64: Which of the following features prevents unauthorized configuration changes to ESXi hosts?

A) Enhanced Linked Mode

B) Lockdown Mode

C) vSphere Replication

D) Role-Based Access Control (RBAC)

Answer: B) Lockdown Mode

Explanation: Lockdown Mode restricts access to ESXi hosts, preventing unauthorized users from making configuration changes directly on the host. Management access must be done through vCenter Server.

Question 65: What does vSphere Encryption provide?

A) It encrypts virtual machine snapshots

B) It encrypts virtual machine data at rest

C) It secures the communication between ESXi hosts

D) It encrypts VM data during live migrations

Answer: B) It encrypts virtual machine data at rest

Explanation: vSphere Encryption is used to secure virtual machine data stored in virtual disks (VMDKs) and ensure that data at rest is protected from unauthorized access.

Automation (Continued)

Question 66: Which of the following PowerCLI cmdlets is used to retrieve information about the storage configuration of ESXi hosts?

A) Get-Datastore

B) Get-VMHostStorage

C) Get-VMHostNetwork

D) Get-VMDisk

Answer: B) Get-VMHostStorage

Explanation: The Get-VMHostStorage cmdlet in PowerCLI is used to retrieve information about the storage configuration for a particular ESXi host. It returns details about storage adapters, devices, and paths. Get-Datastore retrieves datastore information but not the specific storage configurations of the ESXi host.

Question 67: What is the main purpose of the Invoke-VMScript cmdlet in PowerCLI?

A) It configures host-level firewall settings

B) It runs scripts inside a guest operating system of a VM

C) It automatically updates the ESXi host

D) It migrates VMs between different clusters

Answer: B) It runs scripts inside a guest operating system of a VM

Explanation: Invoke-VMScript allows administrators to run scripts or commands inside the guest operating system of a virtual machine from the PowerCLI environment, enabling automation tasks within the VM itself.

Question 68: What is the primary benefit of using the vSphere API?

A) It provides a graphical interface for managing virtual machines

B) It enables programmatic access to automate vSphere features and extend functionality

C) It improves the performance of ESXi hosts

D) It is required for setting up vSphere DRS

Answer: B) It enables programmatic access to automate vSphere features and extend functionality

Explanation: The vSphere API is designed to provide programmatic access to vSphere features, allowing developers and administrators to create custom automation workflows and integrations with third-party tools.

Question 69: Which vSphere API feature allows for integration with modern DevOps and cloud-native tools?

A) SOAP-based API

B) PowerCLI

C) vSphere Automation SDK

D) vSphere FT

Answer: C) vSphere Automation SDK

Explanation: The vSphere Automation SDK provides RESTful APIs and is specifically designed to integrate with modern DevOps and cloud-native tools. It is lighter and more efficient than the older SOAP-based API, making it ideal for cloud-based environments.

Question 70: What does the Set-VMHost cmdlet in PowerCLI allow you to configure?

A) Virtual machine resource settings

B) ESXi host configurations like network and storage settings

C) Datastore size

D) vCenter Server permissions

Answer: B) ESXi host configurations like network and storage settings

Explanation: Set-VMHost allows administrators to configure various settings for an ESXi host, such as networking, storage, and resource allocation. It is useful for automating host-level configurations.

Scenario-Based Questions

Scenario 7: High Availability Configuration

Scenario: You are configuring vSphere HA in a new cluster. The cluster must ensure that all VMs can be restarted in the event of a host failure, and you need to configure Admission Control to ensure enough resources are reserved.

Question: Which Admission Control policy should you configure?

A) Host Failure Cluster Tolerates

B) Restart Priority Policy

C) VM Affinity Rules

D) Proactive HA

Answer: A) Host Failure Cluster Tolerates

Explanation: The Host Failure Cluster Tolerates admission control policy ensures that sufficient resources are reserved in the cluster to accommodate virtual machines in case one or more hosts fail. This guarantees that enough resources are available to restart VMs on the surviving hosts.

Scenario 8: Network Latency Issues

Scenario: A VM is experiencing intermittent network performance issues. You have checked the ESXi host's physical NICs, and they are functioning properly. You suspect the issue might be related to network load balancing in the virtual environment.

Question: Which feature would you use to optimize network traffic distribution?

A) Port Mirroring

B) Network I/O Control (NIOC)

C) Load-Based Teaming (LBT)

D) vMotion

Answer: C) Load-Based Teaming (LBT)

Explanation: Load-Based Teaming (LBT) optimizes the distribution of network traffic across physical NICs based on actual traffic load. It helps ensure that no single NIC is overloaded, improving performance and reducing network congestion for the affected VM.

Scenario 9: Storage Performance Degradation

Scenario: One of the VMs is reporting degraded performance due to high disk I/O latency on an iSCSI datastore. Other VMs are functioning normally on different datastores.

Question: What would be the first step in troubleshooting this issue?

A) Increase the memory allocation to the VM

B) Check the iSCSI network configuration for latency or packet loss

C) Restart the vCenter Server

D) Migrate the VM to a new datastore using Storage vMotion

Answer: B) Check the iSCSI network configuration for latency or packet loss

Explanation: The issue is likely related to storage or network configuration, especially given the use of iSCSI storage. Checking the iSCSI network for latency or packet loss is the first step to diagnose potential performance bottlenecks.

Storage (Continued)

Question 71: What is the primary purpose of vSphere Replication?

A) To mirror VM CPU and memory states

B) To replicate virtual machine data between datastores for disaster recovery

C) To ensure fault tolerance by creating a secondary VM

D) To balance resource usage across hosts

Answer: B) To replicate virtual machine data between datastores for disaster recovery

Explanation: vSphere Replication is used to replicate virtual machine data between different storage locations, allowing for disaster recovery in case the primary storage becomes unavailable.

Question 72: What does vSAN Deduplication and Compression aim to achieve?

A) It reduces the CPU load of VMs

B) It optimizes network traffic between ESXi hosts

C) It reduces the storage footprint of data stored in vSAN clusters

D) It increases virtual machine disk performance

Answer: C) It reduces the storage footprint of data stored in vSAN clusters

Explanation: vSAN Deduplication and Compression is designed to reduce the amount of physical storage space used by eliminating duplicate data and compressing files stored on vSAN datastores. This feature helps optimize storage efficiency.

Question 73: Which of the following describes the vSAN Witness Host in a stretched cluster?

A) A physical host that monitors memory usage

B) A virtual appliance that stores only metadata and quorum information

C) A dedicated backup server

D) A host that mirrors virtual machine storage

Answer: B) A virtual appliance that stores only metadata and quorum information

Explanation: The vSAN Witness Host is used in stretched clusters to store only metadata and quorum information. It does not store actual VM data but helps maintain the integrity of the cluster in case of site failures.

Question 74: What is the main benefit of enabling vSphere Storage DRS?

A) It provides encrypted storage across multiple datastores

B) It balances storage workloads automatically based on performance and capacity

C) It duplicates VMs across multiple hosts

D) It backs up VMs automatically

Answer: B) It balances storage workloads automatically based on performance and capacity

Explanation: Storage DRS monitors datastore capacity and performance and automatically moves virtual machine disk files between datastores to balance workloads and improve performance.

Question 75: In vSphere 8.x, what happens when Storage I/O Control (SIOC) detects high latency on a datastore?

A) SIOC migrates VMs to another datastore

B) SIOC allocates more CPU resources to the affected VMs

C) SIOC prioritizes critical VMs by allocating them more storage resources

D) SIOC reduces the network bandwidth of VMs on the datastore

Answer: C) SIOC prioritizes critical VMs by allocating them more storage resources

Explanation: Storage I/O Control (SIOC) dynamically allocates storage resources to VMs based on their priority, ensuring that critical VMs receive the necessary I/O resources when latency is detected on a shared datastore.

Networking (Continued)

Question 76: What is the primary role of vSphere Distributed Switch (vDS)?

A) It manages network traffic for individual ESXi hosts

B) It provides centralized management of network configurations across multiple ESXi hosts

C) It is used to perform VM migrations between datastores

D) It monitors virtual machine CPU usage

Answer: B) It provides centralized management of network configurations across multiple ESXi hosts

Explanation: vSphere Distributed Switch (vDS) enables centralized network configuration across multiple ESXi hosts, ensuring consistency and simplified management for large-scale environments.

Question 77: What is a VLAN (Virtual Local Area Network) used for in vSphere networking?

A) To balance CPU usage across virtual machines

B) To isolate and segment network traffic within the same physical infrastructure

C) To replicate storage across datastores

D) To create a backup of virtual machine disks

Answer: B) To isolate and segment network traffic within the same physical infrastructure

Explanation: VLANs allow administrators to segment network traffic logically on the same physical infrastructure, improving network security and management by isolating specific types of traffic (e.g., management, storage, and VM traffic).

Question 78: What feature allows for the aggregation of multiple physical NICs to provide failover and load balancing in a vSphere environment?

A) NIC Teaming

B) vSAN

C) Network I/O Control

D) Storage vMotion

Answer: A) NIC Teaming

Explanation: NIC Teaming allows for the aggregation of multiple physical NICs into a single logical interface. It provides redundancy and load balancing, ensuring continuous network availability and optimizing traffic distribution across multiple network interfaces.

Question 79: What is the purpose of a VMkernel Port in vSphere networking?

A) It enables communication between virtual machines on the same host

B) It allows ESXi hosts to connect to storage networks and perform vMotion

C) It provides management access to vCenter Server

D) It duplicates network traffic for monitoring

Answer: B) It allows ESXi hosts to connect to storage networks and perform vMotion

Explanation: A VMkernel Port is used for vSphere services like vMotion, iSCSI storage, NFS storage, and management traffic. It enables hosts to communicate with storage networks and other hosts for tasks like live migrations.

Question 80: Which feature in vSphere Distributed Switch (vDS) allows traffic shaping to manage network bandwidth?

A) Port Mirroring

B) NIOC (Network I/O Control)

C) Load Balancing

D) vSAN

Answer: B) NIOC (Network I/O Control)

Explanation: Network I/O Control (NIOC) allows administrators to define traffic shaping rules for different traffic types (e.g., vMotion, storage, VM traffic) to ensure that critical network traffic gets priority when bandwidth is limited.

Storage (Continued)

Question 81: Which storage technology does VMFS (Virtual Machine File System) use?

A) File-based storage

B) Block-based storage

C) Object-based storage

D) Tape-based storage

Answer: B) Block-based storage

Explanation: VMFS is a block-based storage system designed for use in vSphere environments. It allows multiple ESXi hosts to access the same datastore concurrently and provides the foundation for virtual machine storage.

Question 82: What is the role of the vSAN Disk Group?

A) It aggregates physical storage devices into a logical datastore for VM storage

B) It replicates VM data between multiple hosts

C) It compresses virtual disks to optimize storage

D) It improves VM performance by allocating more CPU resources

Answer: A) It aggregates physical storage devices into a logical datastore for VM storage

Explanation: A vSAN Disk Group combines physical storage devices from an ESXi host into a logical storage unit, forming the basis for the vSAN shared datastore that supports virtual machine storage across the cluster.

Question 83: What is the purpose of Storage vMotion?

A) To migrate virtual machine storage between datastores without downtime

B) To move virtual machines between hosts without migrating their storage

C) To replicate virtual machines to a remote site

D) To back up virtual machine disk files

Answer: A) To migrate virtual machine storage between datastores without downtime

Explanation: Storage vMotion allows for the live migration of virtual machine disk files between datastores without interrupting the virtual machine's operations, enabling maintenance or performance optimization.

Question 84: Which of the following is true about vSAN Stretched Clusters?

A) They provide enhanced storage performance by distributing data across multiple clusters

B) They enable cross-site storage replication and provide failover capabilities between sites

C) They improve the speed of vSphere DRS operations

D) They are limited to a single datacenter

Answer: B) They enable cross-site storage replication and provide failover capabilities between sites

Explanation: vSAN Stretched Clusters provide failover capabilities between geographically separated sites by replicating VM data across different locations, ensuring high availability even in the event of site failures.

Question 85: Which of the following is a benefit of vSAN Deduplication?

A) It reduces CPU overhead for VMs

B) It improves network performance for vMotion operations

C) It minimizes the amount of physical storage required by eliminating duplicate data

D) It increases virtual disk size automatically

Answer: C) It minimizes the amount of physical storage required by eliminating duplicate data

Explanation: vSAN Deduplication reduces the storage footprint by eliminating redundant data blocks, improving storage efficiency, especially in environments with a large number of similar virtual machines.

Security (Continued)

Question 86: Which of the following describes vSphere Role-Based Access Control (RBAC)?

A) It restricts ESXi host access to only local users

B) It assigns permissions to users based on predefined roles and responsibilities

C) It encrypts virtual machine network traffic

D) It creates virtual network firewalls for VMs

Answer: B) It assigns permissions to users based on predefined roles and responsibilities

Explanation: Role-Based Access Control (RBAC) in vSphere assigns permissions to users based on their roles, ensuring that only authorized personnel can perform specific tasks, such as managing VMs, hosts, or datastores.

Question 87: What is the function of vSphere Lockdown Mode?

A) To prevent unauthorized access to ESXi hosts

B) To back up virtual machine configurations

C) To enhance network traffic shaping for VMs

D) To automatically restart failed virtual machines

Answer: A) To prevent unauthorized access to ESXi hosts

Explanation: Lockdown Mode restricts access to ESXi hosts, ensuring that only authorized users can access the host through vCenter Server. It is an important security feature for minimizing attack surfaces on individual hosts.

Question 88: Which type of vSphere encryption protects virtual machine disk files?

A) In-flight encryption

B) At-rest encryption

C) Secure Boot

D) Encrypted vMotion

Answer: B) At-rest encryption

Explanation: At-rest encryption in vSphere protects virtual machine disk files (VMDKs) stored on datastores, ensuring that data is encrypted even when it is not actively being accessed.

Question 89: What is the main use of a Trusted Platform Module (TPM) in a vSphere environment?

A) It ensures secure migration of VMs between hosts

B) It secures the boot process and protects against unauthorized firmware changes

C) It encrypts all network traffic

D) It enables load balancing for virtual machines

Answer: B) It secures the boot process and protects against unauthorized firmware changes

Explanation: TPM is a hardware-based security feature used to protect the boot process and ensure the integrity of ESXi hosts by preventing unauthorized changes to the firmware or OS boot sequence.

Question 90: Which of the following describes the vSphere Certificate Authority (VMCA)?

A) It issues and manages SSL certificates for ESXi hosts and vCenter Server

B) It creates backup copies of VM configurations

C) It replicates VM data across multiple clusters

D) It enables RBAC for virtual machine administration

Answer: A) It issues and manages SSL certificates for ESXi hosts and vCenter Server

Explanation: The vSphere Certificate Authority (VMCA) is responsible for issuing and managing SSL certificates used to secure communication between vSphere components, including ESXi hosts and vCenter Server.

Automation (Continued)

Question 91: What is the purpose of the Get-View cmdlet in PowerCLI?

A) To migrate virtual machines

B) To retrieve detailed information about vSphere objects using the API

C) To start virtual machines on ESXi hosts

D) To back up datastore configurations

Answer: B) To retrieve detailed information about vSphere objects using the API

Explanation: Get-View retrieves low-level, detailed information about vSphere objects, providing access to additional data not available in standard PowerCLI cmdlets. It interacts directly with the vSphere API.

Question 92: What is the use of PowerCLI in a vSphere environment?

A) To configure vCenter Server using the graphical interface

B) To automate tasks and configurations via scripts in a vSphere environment

C) To manage storage I/O control

D) To configure virtual machine encryption

Answer: B) To automate tasks and configurations via scripts in a vSphere environment

Explanation: PowerCLI is a command-line interface tool used to automate various tasks and configurations in a VMware vSphere environment. It is built on PowerShell and allows administrators to automate routine tasks such as provisioning VMs, configuring network settings, and managing storage resources.

Question 93: What is a key feature of vSphere Automation SDK?

A) It is a scripting language for managing networking configurations

B) It provides REST-based API access to VMware vSphere for automation

C) It allows for automatic creation of snapshots in VMs

D) It enables the migration of virtual machines between different clusters

Answer: B) It provides REST-based API access to VMware vSphere for automation

Explanation: The vSphere Automation SDK provides developers with REST-based API access to VMware vSphere, allowing for seamless integration with cloud-native tools and automation of tasks such as provisioning, monitoring, and managing virtual infrastructure.

Question 94: In PowerCLI, which cmdlet is used to move a virtual machine between datastores?

A) Move-VM

B) Get-VM

C) Set-Datastore

D) Get-Datastore

Answer: A) Move-VM

Explanation: Move-VM is the cmdlet used in PowerCLI to move a virtual machine from one datastore to another, or between hosts, enabling administrators to perform migrations, including Storage vMotion, using automated scripts.

Question 95: Which of the following is an advantage of using PowerCLI for virtual machine management?

A) It allows for manual configuration of datastores

B) It automates repetitive tasks like VM creation, management, and performance monitoring

C) It improves storage I/O performance

D) It reduces the need for ESXi host upgrades

Answer: B) It automates repetitive tasks like VM creation, management, and performance monitoring

Explanation: PowerCLI is widely used to automate repetitive tasks such as virtual machine creation, configuration, and performance monitoring. This automation reduces administrative overhead and increases the efficiency of vSphere operations.

Question 96: Which of the following PowerCLI cmdlets retrieves a list of all datastores available in a vCenter Server?

A) Get-Datastore

B) New-VM

C) Get-VMHost

D) Get-VMDatastore

Answer: A) Get-Datastore

Explanation: Get-Datastore is the PowerCLI cmdlet used to retrieve a list of all available datastores in a vSphere environment, providing essential information about the capacity and status of the storage in the infrastructure.

Scenario 10: Automation of VM Deployment

Scenario: An administrator needs to automate the deployment of multiple virtual machines with the same configuration for a development environment. The VM specifications must include 4 vCPUs, 8 GB of RAM, and 100 GB of disk space.

Question: Which PowerCLI cmdlet sequence should the administrator use to automate this process?

A) New-VM, Set-VM, Move-VM

B) New-VM, Set-Datastore, Set-VMHost

C) New-VM, Set-VM, New-HardDisk

D) Get-VM, Get-VMHost, Set-VM

Answer: C) New-VM, Set-VM, New-HardDisk

Explanation: The New-VM cmdlet is used to create the new virtual machines, followed by Set-VM to adjust the virtual machine configurations, and New-HardDisk to allocate the necessary disk space. This ensures that the VMs are configured with the specified resources during deployment.

Storage (Continued)

Question 97: Which of the following is a requirement for configuring vSAN in a vSphere cluster?

A) vSAN can only use NFS-based datastores

B) All ESXi hosts in the cluster must have at least one SSD

C) vSAN requires vMotion to be enabled

D) vSAN is configured automatically with no additional steps

Answer: B) All ESXi hosts in the cluster must have at least one SSD

Explanation: vSAN requires at least one SSD in each ESXi host in the cluster to act as a cache tier for the storage. This SSD is necessary to ensure performance in the vSAN datastore.

Question 98: What is the benefit of enabling vSAN Compression?

A) It compresses virtual machine memory usage

B) It reduces the physical storage footprint by compressing VM data

C) It speeds up network traffic for VMs

D) It improves virtual machine CPU performance

Answer: B) It reduces the physical storage footprint by compressing VM data

Explanation: vSAN Compression reduces the amount of physical storage required by compressing the data stored on the vSAN datastore, increasing storage efficiency without affecting performance.

Question 99: What feature allows vSAN to store data across multiple sites for disaster recovery?

A) vSphere Replication

B) vSAN Stretched Cluster

C) vSphere HA

D) Storage vMotion

Answer: B) vSAN Stretched Cluster

Explanation: A vSAN Stretched Cluster allows for the replication of data across multiple geographic locations, ensuring high availability and enabling disaster recovery in case of site failure.

Question 100: Which of the following is true about vSAN Fault Domains?

A) They replicate data across datastores

B) They are used to ensure data resiliency by placing data across multiple racks or rooms

C) They reduce CPU utilization of VMs

D) They automatically upgrade ESXi hosts in a cluster

Answer: B) They are used to ensure data resiliency by placing data across multiple racks or rooms

Explanation: vSAN Fault Domains allow data to be distributed across different physical locations, such as racks or rooms, ensuring that a failure in one location does not affect the entire cluster's data availability.

Storage (Continued)

Question 101: What is the role of the vSAN Witness in a vSAN Stretched Cluster?

A) It stores backup copies of virtual machine data

B) It provides quorum and ensures data consistency across sites

C) It enhances virtual machine performance by balancing CPU loads

D) It replicates the virtual machine data across multiple datacenters

Answer: B) It provides quorum and ensures data consistency across sites

Explanation: The vSAN Witness in a Stretched Cluster stores only metadata and ensures quorum between sites. It helps maintain data consistency when there are failures or communication issues between the two primary sites.

Question 102: What does the vSAN Storage Policy control?

A) The VM encryption settings across the entire cluster

B) The replication and availability settings of virtual machine storage on vSAN

C) The migration settings for VMs across datastores

D) The CPU allocation for VMs within the cluster

Answer: B) The replication and availability settings of virtual machine storage on vSAN

Explanation: vSAN Storage Policies control how data is stored, replicated, and protected within a vSAN cluster. These policies define the level of redundancy and fault tolerance for the virtual machine's data.

Question 103: Which of the following best describes vSphere Replication?

A) A method for replicating host configurations between datacenters

B) A built-in feature that provides data replication at the VM level for disaster recovery

C) A feature to replicate ESXi host memory for improved performance

D) A backup tool that stores virtual machine snapshots in a remote location

Answer: B) A built-in feature that provides data replication at the VM level for disaster recovery

Explanation: vSphere Replication is a built-in feature that allows for the replication of virtual machine data at the VM level. It is commonly used in disaster recovery scenarios to ensure that VMs can be restored at a secondary site if the primary site fails.

Question 104: What is the role of Storage I/O Control (SIOC) in vSphere?

A) To prioritize virtual machine CPU resources based on demand

B) To monitor and control storage I/O across shared datastores

C) To create snapshots of virtual machines

D) To backup data to a remote datastore

Answer: B) To monitor and control storage I/O across shared datastores

Explanation: Storage I/O Control (SIOC) dynamically manages and controls storage input/output operations on shared datastores, ensuring that critical VMs receive sufficient storage resources when contention occurs.

Question 105: What does Storage DRS use to balance virtual machine storage?

A) Datastore replication

B) Latency and capacity thresholds

C) Network traffic shaping

D) Fault tolerance mechanisms

Answer: B) Latency and capacity thresholds

Explanation: Storage DRS uses both latency and capacity thresholds to balance the storage of virtual machines across datastores. It automatically moves VMs to improve performance and avoid overloading a single datastore.

Security (Continued)

Question 106: What is the primary benefit of using vSphere VM Encryption?

A) It speeds up VM migrations

B) It secures VM data at rest by encrypting VMDKs

C) It improves network performance for encrypted VMs

D) It automatically backs up VMs to a remote datastore

Answer: B) It secures VM data at rest by encrypting VMDKs

Explanation: vSphere VM Encryption protects virtual machine data at rest by encrypting the virtual disks (VMDKs). It ensures that data stored in datastores is protected from unauthorized access.

Question 107: How does vSphere Lockdown Mode improve security?

A) By encrypting all data traffic between VMs

B) By restricting direct access to ESXi hosts

C) By requiring encryption for all storage devices

D) By automatically applying security patches to all VMs

Answer: B) By restricting direct access to ESXi hosts

Explanation: vSphere Lockdown Mode enhances security by limiting direct access to ESXi hosts. When enabled, all host management must be done through vCenter Server, reducing potential attack vectors.

Question 108: Which feature allows for the encryption of virtual machine live migrations in vSphere?

A) vSAN

B) Encrypted vMotion

C) DRS

D) vSphere HA

Answer: B) Encrypted vMotion

Explanation: Encrypted vMotion secures the migration of virtual machines between hosts by encrypting the data in transit, ensuring that sensitive information is protected during live migrations.

Question 109: What does the vSphere Trust Authority (vTA) provide?

A) Role-based access control for administrators

B) Encryption of network traffic between virtual machines

C) Hardware-based security for ensuring the integrity of the vSphere infrastructure

D) A tool for monitoring resource consumption in the vCenter Server

Answer: C) Hardware-based security for ensuring the integrity of the vSphere infrastructure

Explanation: vSphere Trust Authority (vTA) enhances security by using hardware-based security modules, like TPM (Trusted Platform Module), to ensure the integrity of the ESXi hosts and vCenter Server infrastructure.

Question 110: Which vSphere feature ensures that only signed and trusted code is loaded during the boot process?

A) Secure Boot

B) vSphere FT

C) vSphere HA

D) vSAN Encryption

Answer: A) Secure Boot

Explanation: Secure Boot ensures that only signed and trusted code is loaded during the boot process of ESXi hosts, helping prevent unauthorized or malicious software from running.

Automation (Continued)

Question 111: Which PowerCLI cmdlet is used to create a snapshot of a virtual machine?

A) New-Snapshot

B) Set-VM

C) Get-VM

D) New-VMHost

Answer: A) New-Snapshot

Explanation: New-Snapshot is the PowerCLI cmdlet used to create snapshots of virtual machines, allowing administrators to save the state of a VM at a specific point in time for backup or testing purposes.

Question 112: What is the function of Set-VMHost in PowerCLI?

A) It creates a new VM in the host

B) It configures ESXi host settings like networking and storage

C) It migrates VMs to another datastore

D) It retrieves a list of all hosts in the vCenter Server

Answer: B) It configures ESXi host settings like networking and storage

Explanation: Set-VMHost is used in PowerCLI to configure ESXi host settings, such as networking, storage, and resource allocation, enabling automated management of the host infrastructure.

Question 113: In PowerCLI, what is the purpose of the Move-VM cmdlet?

A) It backs up virtual machines to a remote location

B) It migrates virtual machines between hosts or datastores

C) It restores snapshots of virtual machines

D) It replicates VMs between different vCenter Servers

Answer: B) It migrates virtual machines between hosts or datastores

Explanation: Move-VM is the PowerCLI cmdlet used to migrate VMs between hosts or datastores, making it useful for performing live migrations, including vMotion and Storage vMotion operations.

Question 114: Which API provides developers with a modern, REST-based interface for automating vSphere management?

A) vSphere Web Client API

B) vSphere SOAP API

C) vSphere Automation API

D) PowerCLI

Answer: C) vSphere Automation API

Explanation: The vSphere Automation API provides a modern, REST-based interface for automating and integrating vSphere with other tools and systems. It simplifies automation by allowing developers to interact with vSphere programmatically using standard HTTP requests.

Question 115: What does Invoke-VMScript in PowerCLI allow administrators to do?

A) Restart ESXi hosts from the command line

B) Run scripts inside a guest OS on a virtual machine

C) Automate the migration of VMs between clusters

D) Generate reports on virtual machine performance

Answer: B) Run scripts inside a guest OS on a virtual machine

Explanation: Invoke-VMScript allows administrators to run scripts directly within the guest operating system of a virtual machine, providing a powerful way to automate tasks inside the VM from outside the OS.

Storage (Continued)

Question 116: What is the role of the vSAN Witness Host in a vSAN Stretched Cluster?

A) To store VM data for additional redundancy

B) To provide quorum for maintaining cluster integrity in case of site failure

C) To replicate VM snapshots across the cluster

D) To balance resource utilization across ESXi hosts

Answer: B) To provide quorum for maintaining cluster integrity in case of site failure

Explanation: The vSAN Witness Host provides quorum, ensuring that the vSAN Stretched Cluster can maintain data consistency and operation even if one site goes down. It does not store VM data but stores metadata needed for maintaining quorum and availability.

Question 117: What is the key benefit of vSAN All-Flash configurations?

A) Increased CPU performance

B) Lower storage latency and higher IOPS compared to hybrid configurations

C) Automatic encryption of all data at rest

D) Decreased memory usage in virtual machines

Answer: B) Lower storage latency and higher IOPS compared to hybrid configurations

Explanation: vSAN All-Flash configurations offer significantly lower storage latency and higher IOPS (Input/Output Operations Per Second) compared to hybrid configurations, which combine SSDs for caching and HDDs for capacity.

Question 118: Which vSphere feature allows for cross-vCenter vMotion operations?

A) vSphere Replication

B) Cross-vCenter vMotion

C) vSAN Fault Tolerance

D) vSphere HA

Answer: B) Cross-vCenter vMotion

Explanation: Cross-vCenter vMotion allows for the migration of virtual machines across vCenter Server instances without any downtime. This feature is useful for seamless VM mobility across different data centers or geographic locations.

Question 119: In vSAN, what is the purpose of the capacity tier in a disk group?

A) To replicate VM memory across hosts

B) To store the actual virtual machine data

C) To cache frequently accessed data for performance

D) To replicate host configuration data

Answer: B) To store the actual virtual machine data

Explanation: In vSAN, the capacity tier is used to store the actual virtual machine data, while the cache tier (typically SSDs) is used to accelerate read/write operations and improve performance.

Question 120: What happens if a vSAN cluster loses connectivity to the vSAN Witness Host?

A) The cluster will continue functioning normally without interruption

B) The cluster can still function, but quorum decisions cannot be made

C) The cluster data will be immediately encrypted

D) All VM data will be replicated to the secondary site automatically

Answer: B) The cluster can still function, but quorum decisions cannot be made

Explanation: If a vSAN Stretched Cluster loses connectivity to the Witness Host, the cluster can still function for a time, but if a failure occurs, quorum decisions cannot be made, potentially leading to split-brain scenarios.

Security (Continued)

Question 121: What is the purpose of vSphere Secure Boot?

A) It automates the backup of virtual machines

B) It ensures that only digitally signed and trusted code is loaded during the boot process

C) It enables faster VM migration between hosts

D) It provides automatic VM snapshot creation during boot

Answer: B) It ensures that only digitally signed and trusted code is loaded during the boot process

Explanation: Secure Boot helps to protect the integrity of the ESXi host by ensuring that only digitally signed, trusted code and drivers are loaded during the boot process.

Question 122: What is the function of vSphere Certificate Management?

A) To manage SSL certificates used to secure communication between vSphere components

B) To manage encryption keys for virtual machines

C) To automate VM migration across different vCenters

D) To manage role-based access controls for ESXi hosts

Answer: A) To manage SSL certificates used to secure communication between vSphere components

Explanation: vSphere Certificate Management manages the SSL certificates used to secure communication between different vSphere components such as ESXi hosts, vCenter Servers, and other services.

Question 123: Which of the following is used to secure the boot process on ESXi hosts?

A) Encrypted vMotion

B) vSphere FT

C) Secure Boot

D) vSAN Encryption

Answer: C) Secure Boot

Explanation: Secure Boot secures the boot process by ensuring that only trusted and signed code is loaded during ESXi host boot. This prevents tampering and ensures the integrity of the host.

Question 124: How does vSphere Trust Authority (vTA) enhance security?

A) By encrypting all data traffic between VMs

B) By creating a trusted infrastructure using hardware-backed security features

C) By monitoring VM resource usage

D) By enabling automatic VM recovery in case of failure

Answer: B) By creating a trusted infrastructure using hardware-backed security features

Explanation: vSphere Trust Authority (vTA) enhances security by leveraging hardware-based security modules such as TPM (Trusted Platform Module) to ensure the integrity and security of the ESXi host and vCenter infrastructure.

Question 125: Which feature in vSphere enables Encrypted vMotion?

A) vSphere HA

B) vSphere DRS

C) VM Encryption

D) vSphere 6.5 and above with vCenter Server and ESXi 6.5+

Answer: D) vSphere 6.5 and above with vCenter Server and ESXi 6.5+

Explanation: Encrypted vMotion is available starting from vSphere 6.5, and it encrypts the data transmitted during live VM migrations (vMotion) to protect sensitive information from being intercepted during the migration process.

Automation (Continued)

Question 126: In PowerCLI, which cmdlet would you use to retrieve information about virtual machines?

A) Set-VM

B) Get-VM

C) Move-VM

D) New-VM

Answer: B) Get-VM

Explanation: Get-VM is the cmdlet used in PowerCLI to retrieve information about virtual machines, such as their status, configuration, and resource allocation.

Question 127: What is the benefit of using PowerCLI for vSphere management?

A) It provides a graphical user interface for managing VMs

B) It automates tasks such as provisioning, configuring, and managing virtual infrastructure

C) It improves CPU performance on ESXi hosts

D) It automatically patches virtual machines

Answer: B) It automates tasks such as provisioning, configuring, and managing virtual infrastructure

Explanation: PowerCLI is a powerful automation tool for managing vSphere environments through scripting. It automates various tasks such as creating VMs, configuring hosts, managing resources, and generating reports.

Question 128: Which PowerCLI cmdlet is used to configure networking on an ESXi host?

A) Set-VM

B) Set-VMHostNetworkAdapter

C) Get-VMHostNetwork

D) New-Datastore

Answer: B) Set-VMHostNetworkAdapter

Explanation: Set-VMHostNetworkAdapter is the PowerCLI cmdlet used to configure the network settings of ESXi hosts, such as assigning IP addresses, VLANs, and NIC teaming options.

Question 129: What does the Move-VM cmdlet do in PowerCLI?

A) It migrates virtual machines between datastores or hosts

B) It retrieves performance data for virtual machines

C) It creates a new VM snapshot

D) It automates the deployment of vCenter Server

Answer: A) It migrates virtual machines between datastores or hosts

Explanation: Move-VM is the PowerCLI cmdlet used to migrate virtual machines between hosts or datastores, enabling administrators to perform live migrations (vMotion or Storage vMotion) through automation.

Question 130: Which PowerCLI cmdlet is used to create a new virtual machine?

A) New-VM

B) Set-VMHost

C) Get-VMHost

D) Move-VM

Answer: A) New-VM

Explanation: New-VM is the PowerCLI cmdlet used to create a new virtual machine. Administrators can specify various parameters, such as CPU, memory, and storage configurations, to automate the deployment of VMs.

Storage (Continued)

Question 131: What is the purpose of the vSAN Performance Service?

A) To automatically replicate data across datastores

B) To monitor and analyze vSAN performance metrics such as IOPS, throughput, and latency

C) To migrate VMs across clusters without downtime

D) To increase the virtual machine memory allocation automatically

Answer: B) To monitor and analyze vSAN performance metrics such as IOPS, throughput, and latency

Explanation: The vSAN Performance Service is used to monitor and analyze storage performance in vSAN environments, providing metrics such as IOPS, throughput, and latency to help administrators optimize performance and troubleshoot issues.

Question 132: In a vSAN Stretched Cluster, what happens when a single site fails?

A) All virtual machines are shut down

B) Virtual machines continue running from the other site without downtime

C) vSphere HA restarts the virtual machines on another cluster

D) The vSAN Witness Host takes over all virtual machine operations

Answer: B) Virtual machines continue running from the other site without downtime

Explanation: In a vSAN Stretched Cluster, if one site fails, virtual machines continue to run from the surviving site without downtime, thanks to the redundancy and replication of data between the sites.

Question 133: What is the primary use of vSAN Data-at-Rest Encryption?

A) To encrypt VM memory during migrations

B) To encrypt all data stored on vSAN disks for security

C) To encrypt network traffic between ESXi hosts

D) To encrypt only the virtual machine configuration files

Answer: B) To encrypt all data stored on vSAN disks for security

Explanation: vSAN Data-at-Rest Encryption encrypts all data stored on vSAN disks, protecting virtual machine data from unauthorized access, even if the physical disks are removed or stolen.

Question 134: Which of the following best describes vSphere Thin Provisioning?

A) It pre-allocates all storage space for virtual machines

B) It dynamically allocates storage space to virtual machines as needed

C) It compresses storage used by virtual machines

D) It automatically backs up virtual machines when disk usage increases

Answer: B) It dynamically allocates storage space to virtual machines as needed

Explanation: Thin Provisioning dynamically allocates storage space to VMs only when needed, allowing for better utilization of available storage by not pre-allocating all disk space upfront.

Question 135: In vSAN, what is the function of a Fault Domain?

A) To provide additional storage capacity in the cluster

B) To isolate and protect data by distributing it across different physical locations, such as racks or rooms

C) To enhance CPU performance for high-priority virtual machines

D) To automatically back up virtual machines to a remote location

Answer: B) To isolate and protect data by distributing it across different physical locations, such as racks or rooms

Explanation: Fault Domains in vSAN are used to distribute data across different physical locations (e.g., racks or rooms) to protect against data loss from hardware failures affecting an entire rack or site.

Security (Continued)

Question 136: What does vSphere Role-Based Access Control (RBAC) allow administrators to do?

A) Automate the configuration of vSphere components

B) Assign different levels of access and permissions based on user roles

C) Enforce encryption on all datastores

D) Prevent virtual machines from migrating across hosts

Answer: B) Assign different levels of access and permissions based on user roles

Explanation: Role-Based Access Control (RBAC) in vSphere enables administrators to assign different levels of permissions to users based on their roles, ensuring that users can only access resources and perform tasks for which they are authorized.

Question 137: How does VM Encryption in vSphere help protect virtual machine data?

A) By encrypting all VM data at rest, preventing unauthorized access

B) By automatically replicating VM data to another site

C) By creating backup snapshots of encrypted VMs

D) By encrypting VM memory and CPU resources

Answer: A) By encrypting all VM data at rest, preventing unauthorized access

Explanation: VM Encryption secures all virtual machine data at rest by encrypting the virtual disks (VMDKs). This ensures that unauthorized users cannot access the data, even if they gain access to the underlying storage.

Question 138: Which of the following is a requirement for enabling vSphere VM Encryption?

A) vCenter Server and ESXi must be configured with a Key Management Server (KMS)

B) All virtual machines must use thin provisioning

C) Virtual machines must be part of a stretched cluster

D) ESXi hosts must have at least 64 GB of RAM

Answer: A) vCenter Server and ESXi must be configured with a Key Management Server (KMS)

Explanation: To enable VM Encryption in vSphere, you must configure a Key Management Server (KMS) in vCenter Server and ESXi. The KMS handles the encryption keys necessary for encrypting and decrypting VM data.

Question 139: What is the purpose of vSphere Trust Authority (vTA)?

A) To monitor virtual machine performance

B) To establish a hardware-based trusted infrastructure using TPM and attestation

C) To manage VM snapshots and backups

D) To automatically encrypt all network traffic between hosts

Answer: B) To establish a hardware-based trusted infrastructure using TPM and attestation

Explanation: vSphere Trust Authority (vTA) leverages hardware-backed security features like TPM (Trusted Platform Module) to ensure that only trusted hardware and software are running in the vSphere environment.

Question 140: Which feature ensures that only signed and trusted code is loaded during the boot process of an ESXi host?

A) Lockdown Mode

B) Secure Boot

C) Fault Tolerance

D) Encrypted vMotion

Answer: B) Secure Boot

Explanation: Secure Boot ensures that only signed and trusted code, including drivers and firmware, is loaded during the boot process of an ESXi host. This feature helps maintain the integrity and security of the ESXi environment.

Automation (Continued)

Question 141: Which PowerCLI cmdlet is used to create a new virtual machine?

A) Set-VM

B) Get-VM

C) New-VM

D) Move-VM

Answer: C) New-VM

Explanation: New-VM is the PowerCLI cmdlet used to create new virtual machines. Administrators can define the number of CPUs, memory, storage, and other properties using this cmdlet.

Question 142: What is the purpose of the Get-VMHost cmdlet in PowerCLI?

A) To retrieve a list of all virtual machines

B) To retrieve a list of ESXi hosts and their properties

C) To migrate virtual machines between hosts

D) To restart virtual machines across clusters

Answer: B) To retrieve a list of ESXi hosts and their properties

Explanation: Get-VMHost is the PowerCLI cmdlet used to retrieve a list of ESXi hosts, along with details about their configurations, status, and resource usage.

Question 143: What does the Set-VM cmdlet in PowerCLI allow administrators to do?

A) Create a new datastore for a VM

B) Configure virtual machine properties such as CPU, memory, and network adapters

C) Encrypt a virtual machine's storage

D) Automate the migration of VMs between clusters

Answer: B) Configure virtual machine properties such as CPU, memory, and network adapters

Explanation: Set-VM is the PowerCLI cmdlet used to modify virtual machine properties, including CPU, memory, storage, and network settings.

Question 144: What is the primary function of the Move-VM cmdlet in PowerCLI?

A) To automate snapshots for multiple VMs

B) To migrate virtual machines between hosts or datastores

C) To back up virtual machine configurations

D) To encrypt virtual machine disk files

Answer: B) To migrate virtual machines between hosts or datastores

Explanation: Move-VM is the PowerCLI cmdlet that allows administrators to migrate virtual machines between hosts or datastores, enabling vMotion or Storage vMotion operations through automation.

Question 145: Which API offers a REST-based interface for automating vSphere management?

A) vSphere Web Client API

B) SOAP API

C) vSphere Automation API

D) PowerCLI

Answer: C) vSphere Automation API

Explanation: The vSphere Automation API provides a modern, REST-based interface for automating vSphere management tasks, making it easier to integrate with cloud-native applications and DevOps tools.

Scenario-Based Questions

Scenario 11: Virtual Machine Performance Issue

Scenario: A virtual machine is experiencing high CPU contention, and you want to improve performance by adjusting its configuration. You notice that the VM has been assigned more vCPUs than necessary for its workload.

Question: What would be the recommended approach to optimize performance?

A) Increase the number of vCPUs

B) Decrease the number of vCPUs to better match the workload

C) Enable Storage I/O Control (SIOC) for the VM

D) Enable Fault Tolerance for the VM

Answer: B) Decrease the number of vCPUs to better match the workload

Explanation: Over-provisioning vCPUs can lead to CPU contention issues as multiple virtual CPUs compete for physical CPU resources. Reducing the number of vCPUs to a level that matches the VM's workload can help improve performance by reducing unnecessary competition for CPU time. Increasing the number of vCPUs (Option A) would likely worsen the issue, while enabling SIOC or Fault Tolerance (Options C and D) does not directly address CPU contention problems.

Scenario 12: Host Failure in a vSphere Cluster

Scenario: One of the hosts in your vSphere cluster has failed, and you need to ensure that the virtual machines are restarted on another host without manual intervention.

Question: Which vSphere feature will automatically restart the VMs on another host after a host failure?

A) vSphere Replication

B) vSphere HA

C) vSphere DRS

D) vSphere FT

Answer: B) vSphere HA

Explanation: vSphere High Availability (HA) is designed to detect host failures and automatically restart the virtual machines on other hosts in the cluster. vSphere DRS (Option C) helps balance resource usage but is not responsible for handling host failures. vSphere Replication (Option A) is used for disaster recovery replication, and Fault Tolerance (FT) (Option D) provides continuous availability for critical workloads but does not apply to all VMs.

Networking (Continued)

Question 146: What is the main purpose of Network I/O Control (NIOC) in a vSphere environment?

A) To automatically back up network settings

B) To prioritize and allocate network bandwidth based on traffic type

C) To encrypt all network traffic between hosts

D) To enable vMotion between different clusters

Answer: B) To prioritize and allocate network bandwidth based on traffic type

Explanation: Network I/O Control (NIOC) allows administrators to define traffic classes and allocate bandwidth based on the priority of each traffic type (e.g., VM traffic, vMotion, management traffic), ensuring that critical traffic gets priority when network resources are constrained.

Question 147: Which feature of vSphere Distributed Switch (vDS) allows traffic shaping to control the flow of data in and out of the virtual switch?

A) Port Mirroring

B) Load-Based Teaming

C) Network I/O Control (NIOC)

D) Traffic Shaping

Answer: D) Traffic Shaping

Explanation: Traffic Shaping on a vSphere Distributed Switch (vDS) allows administrators to control the amount of network bandwidth used by virtual machines by setting limits on the average and peak data rates. This helps manage network traffic flow, particularly during peak usage times.

Question 148: What is the function of a VMkernel Port?

A) To provide network access for virtual machines

B) To enable ESXi hosts to communicate for vSphere services such as vMotion and iSCSI storage

C) To replicate data between hosts in a vSAN cluster

D) To connect virtual machines to the internet

Answer: B) To enable ESXi hosts to communicate for vSphere services such as vMotion and iSCSI storage

Explanation: A VMkernel Port is used by ESXi hosts for internal communication between hosts and for services like vMotion, iSCSI, NFS, and management traffic. It is essential for the operation of key vSphere features.

Question 149: What happens when vSphere Storage I/O Control (SIOC) detects high latency on a shared datastore?

A) It migrates virtual machines to another datastore

B) It allocates more storage I/O resources to higher-priority virtual machines

C) It shuts down non-critical virtual machines

D) It increases CPU resources for storage traffic

Answer: B) It allocates more storage I/O resources to higher-priority virtual machines

Explanation: SIOC monitors the latency on shared datastores and dynamically adjusts I/O resource allocation based on the priority of the virtual machines, ensuring that critical workloads receive the necessary I/O resources when the datastore is congested.

Question 150: Which feature enables live migration of virtual machines between hosts without downtime?

A) vSAN

B) vMotion

C) vSphere Replication

D) vSphere HA

Answer: B) vMotion

Explanation: vMotion allows for the live migration of virtual machines between hosts with no downtime, ensuring that workloads can be moved seamlessly for maintenance, load balancing, or other reasons without affecting end-users or applications.

Made in United States
Orlando, FL
09 May 2025

61140865R00129